BAY AREA BIKE RIDES

BAY AREA
BIKE RIDES

RAY HOSLER
3RD. EDITION

CHRONICLE BOOKS
SAN FRANCISCO

Third Edition

Cover photograph: © 2000 Harold Sund/The Image Bank
Cover design: Aya Akazawa
Interior design: Pamela Geismar
Composition: Candace Creasy, Blue Friday Type & Graphics
Fonts: Solex, ITC Century, Trade Gothic

Library of Congress Cataloging-in-Publication Data:
Hosler, Ray.
    Bay area bike rides / by Ray Hosler. —Third ed.
       p. cm.
    Includes index.
    ISBN 0-8118-3421-2
1. Bicycle touring—California—San Francisco Bay Area—Guidebooks.
2. San Francisco Bay Area (Calif.)—Guidebooks. I. Title.
GV1045.5.C22 S264 2002
    917.94'60454—dc21   2001042219

Manufactured in the United States of America.

Distributed in Canada by Raincoast Books
9050 Shaughnessy Street
Vancouver, British Columbia V6P 6E5

10 9 8 7 6 5 4 3 2

Chronicle Books LLC
85 Second Street
San Francisco, California 94105

www.chroniclebooks.com

ACKNOWLEDGMENTS

A heartfelt thanks goes to the following individuals who helped me research, edit, and write *Bay Area Bike Rides*: Jobst Brandt, for leading the way on rides and giving editorial advice; Michael Kelley, for leading rides in the East Bay; Jim Westby, for loaning his mountain bike; Ted Mock, Mark Levine, Gary Flint, Joe Terhar, Ray Mengel, Mike Johnston, and others for riding along; Joe Breeze, for the Mt. Tamalpais mountain bike ride; John Schubert in Guerneville; Gage McKinney and Dick Wachs in San Jose; and all the government agencies and libraries that provided invaluable information, some of it on the Internet. Long live the Internet.

Contents

Introduction

BICYCLING IN THE SAN FRANCISCO BAY AREA HAS SOMETHING FOR EVERY-one—quiet country roads close to an urban setting, mountains, bay-lands, the Pacific Ocean. It's all nearby. Such diversity makes this area, on the whole, the world's best bike-riding location. After twenty-four years of bicycling here, I still find new adventure. And many an adventure I've had: clambering over downed redwoods on Gazos Creek after the floods of 1982–83; riding into fluffy white fog and damp, cool canyons by the ocean on sweltering hot days; cycling down the face of Mt. Diablo on a roller-coaster trail; seeing wild boar in remote sections of Henry W. Coe State Park; moonlight rides over Dumbarton Bridge and up Mt. Hamilton.

Although the Bay Area has its share of traffic, your bicycling experience can be car-free and carefree with many of the rides I've mapped. Most rides can be reached within one hour by car, or by taking Bay Area Rapid Transit, a ferry, or even a bus. Consider the possibilities: Take the ferry from San Francisco to Sausalito, then bicycle to Muir Woods National Monument. Stroll through the park's majestic redwood groves. Then cycle home over the inspiring Golden Gate Bridge or return by ferry.

In the Bay Area, we ride year-round. Each season has something to offer. In the spring I like to ride over Mt. Hamilton to see wildflowers. In the summer there's nothing more refreshing than a cool ride on the foggy Pacific Coast. In the fall, trees display crimson reds and golden yellows in the Santa Cruz Mountains. In the winter I often ride to the bay for bird-watching or visit local parks to hike and ride.

No matter what the season, be prepared to pay homage to the Bay Area's weather gods. Their moods change by the hour and by the mile, especially between bay and ocean, and low and high elevations. It can be hot one minute and cold the next. On cold days I've ridden through pockets of hot air in secluded canyons.

Even less predictable than the weather are motorists. Always be alert for sudden and unexpected maneuvers from cars. Never assume drivers know what you're doing, either. Although car encounters are few and far between for most cyclists, remember that you're not the only person using the road. Ride single file on all roads—this isn't Italy, where the bike is king. You're better off avoiding confrontations with motorists. Unless you're looking for trouble, ignore rude or inattentive drivers.

No doubt, some roads I've chosen here have changed or will change after the book is published. They'll be torn up, repaved, or even closed. Mountain bike trails will be opened, renamed, rerouted, or prohibited for riding. Since the first edition, the Bay Area has weathered a major earthquake, a devastating fire, and a drought. That's why you should always check with a local bicycle shop about road conditions. The book's maps include other interesting roads you can take, if you run into detours. It's also a good idea to check with a park ranger to see which trails are open to bicycles. Some trails are closed in wet weather.

Off-road riding calls for many of the same precautions as road riding, only you are the "motorist" on the trails, and it's your responsibility to watch out for hikers and equestrians. Fortunately, off-road riding has won the respect of park officials, who were wary in the early years of the mountain bike. Many mountain bikers ride responsibly and help maintain trails, working closely with government agencies and trail groups. However, some riders continue to flout the law, build illegal trails, and ride recklessly. I know only too well. In 1995 a "Rambo" mountain biker slammed into me head-on, knocking me unconscious and damaging my bike. Ride safely and responsibly, or trails will be closed to us again.

Bicycles are permitted on narrow hiking trails in a few Bay Area locations. The "trails" shown in the off-road rides are mostly old logging or service roads designated for mixed use. Ride no faster than 15 mph and pass other trail users at reduced speed, usually 5 mph or less. But most important, control your bike at all times and be able to stop in a short distance. Note that Santa Clara County requires bicyclists to wear helmets in many of its parks, and helmets are required on all Midpeninsula Regional Open Space District land. To avoid disappointment, be on the safe side and wear a helmet.

The book is divided into three sections: mountain bike rides, road rides, and casual rides. Mountain bike rides are on mostly dirt. Road rides stay on pavement. Casual rides are flat and located in parks and recreation areas where you can stay on recreation paths away from traffic. Use caution passing pedestrians, and don't exceed 10 mph when other trail users are present.

Most of the Bay Area's rural roads were built between 1850 and 1890 for logging and commerce. The course chosen by the road builders sometimes followed trails used by Native Americans. Other roads were built for special purposes, like the road up Mt. Hamilton, which was constructed for the summit's telescope observatory. Parts of Highway 9 and Highway 236 were built in the early 1900s to connect Big Basin Redwoods State Park with Santa Clara Valley. More recently, multi-use paths have emerged from railroad rights-of-way.

I wrote this book to include something for everyone—hilly, mountainous, and flat rides. With the proper gears and conditioning, most of the rides can be accomplished by cyclists of all ages and abilities. Rides were measured using an Avocet cyclometer and noting turns, rest stops, and points of interest. A cyclometer and Mileage Log will reduce the chance of getting lost. Cyclometers aren't as accurate on dirt roads, so pay attention to the map, as your mileage may vary.

Finally, this third edition includes a section with links to Web sites that give information on parks and other places of interest. In the years since the last edition, the Web has turned into a priceless resource. It's a virtual community, allowing bicyclists around the world to share information. Enough said. Let's go for a bike ride.

Bicycles on Public Transit

Bicycles may be taken on BART, bay ferries, Caltrain, most buses, and light rail in the San Francisco Bay Area. Restrictions apply and may change without notice, so check with the agencies listed here before using them.

BAY AREA RAPID TRANSIT (BART). Bicycles are allowed at most times of the day. Use common sense during rush hour. San Francisco phone (415) 989-2278. BART bicycle rules: www.transitinfo.org/BART/bicycles.html

SAN FRANCISCO MUNI. Bike racks have been installed on Muni routes 17, 35, 36, 37, 39, 53, 56, 66, 76, and 91. Bikes are not allowed on any other route. Phone (415) 673-MUNI (6864). www.transitinfo.org/Muni/bicycles.html

CALTRAIN. Caltrain, which runs between San Francisco and Gilroy, has accommodations for bicycles only in the car closest to San Francisco (two cars on some schedules). One car holds a maximum of 24 bikes. Bicycles are allowed on every train, every day. Phone (800) 660-4287. Caltrain bicycle rules: www.transitinfo.org/Caltrain/bicycles.html

SANTA CLARA VALLEY TRANSPORTATION AUTHORITY (VTA). Bicycles—up to two per bus—are permitted on all buses in Santa Clara County, but only when there is room available and at the discretion of the driver. Operators cannot leave the bus to assist boarding. Phone (800) 894-9908.

SAN JOSE LIGHT RAIL. Extending from south San Jose to Mountain View, the light rail allows up to six bicycles per car. Phone (800) 894-9908. VTA bicycle rules: www.transitinfo.org/SCVTA/bicycles.html

BAY FERRY SERVICE. All San Francisco Bay ferries servicing Alameda, Sausalito, Larkspur, Tiburon, Richmond, San Francisco, Oakland, and Vallejo permit bicycles free. Most of the ferry services are operated by Golden Gate Ferry Service. Phone (415) 257-4563.

Alameda/Oakland Ferry Service operates between Oakland and San Francisco. Phone (510) 522-3300. www.eastbayferry.com

Harbor Bay Island Ferry operates between Alameda and San Francisco. Phone (510) 769-5500. www.harborbay.com/hbm/pages/ferry.htm

Larkspur Ferry provides service between Larkspur and San Francisco seven days a week. www.transitinfo.org/Sched/GF/LARK/A

Blue and Gold Fleet operates Monday through Friday between Sausalito and Tiburon and San Francisco's Ferry Building. Phone (415) 773-1188. www.blueandgoldfleet.com

Red and White Fleet operates between Richmond and San Francisco. Phone (415) 447-0597. www.redandwhite.com

Baylinks Ferry operates between Vallejo and San Francisco. Phone (707) 648-4666. www.baylinkferry.com

AC TRANSIT (ALAMEDA AND CONTRA COSTA TRANSIT AUTHORITY). On selected trips and on specific routes only, AC Transit buses are equipped with front-mounted bike racks that hold two bicycles at a time. Phone (510) 839-2882. Bicycle rules: www.transitinfo.org/AC/bicycles.html

SAMTRANS. San Mateo County buses have racks for two bicycles. Only single-rider, two-wheel bicycles are permitted. No motor, tandem, or three-wheel bikes are allowed. There is no age limit for riders using the bike racks or bringing bikes on board the bus. However, riders must be able to load and unload their bikes without help from the operator. Phone (800) 660-4287. Bicycle rules: www.transitinfo.org/SamTrans/bicycles.html

COUNTY CONNECTION. Buses in Contra Costa County have a bicycle rack at the front that holds two bikes. Phone (925) 676-7500. www. transitinfo.org/CC/bicycles.html

For more information about bicycle organizations, bikes on Bay Area bridges, public bike lockers, and bicycles on public transit, contact the Regional Bicycle Advisory Committee (REBAC), P.O. Box 10205, Oakland, CA 94610. Phone (510) 452-1221 during business hours. www.bayareabikes.org

For San Francisco Bay Area Transit Information: www.transitinfo. org

Bike Clubs

WESTERN WHEELERS (Palo Alto): www.westernwheelers.org

ALMADEN CYCLE TOURING CLUB (South Bay): www.actc.org

GRIZZLY PEAK CYCLISTS (Berkeley): www.grizzlypeakcyclists.org

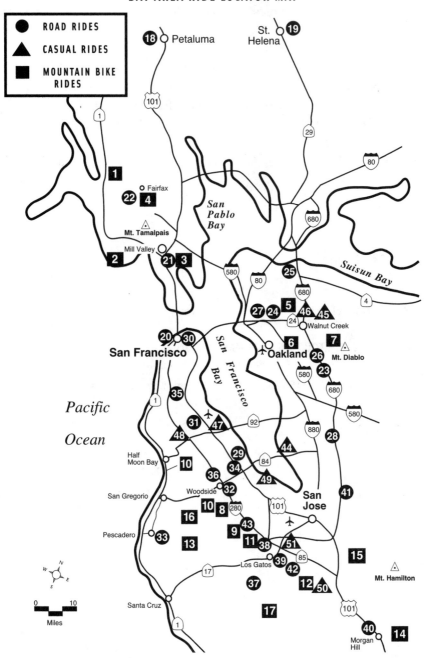

BAY AREA RIDE LOCATOR MAP

Legend:
- ● ROAD RIDES
- ▲ CASUAL RIDES
- ■ MOUNTAIN BIKE RIDES

Petaluma
St. Helena
Fairfax
San Pablo Bay
Mt. Tamalpais
Mill Valley
Suisun Bay
Walnut Creek
San Francisco
Oakland
Mt. Diablo
Pacific Ocean
San Francisco Bay
Half Moon Bay
San Gregorio
Woodside
San Jose
Pescadero
Los Gatos
Santa Cruz
Mt. Hamilton
Morgan Hill

Miles
0   10

N
W   E
S

KEY TO MAPS

Airport	✈	Oil well	🛢
Altitude, point of interest	●	Old-growth redwoods, unusual tree	🌲
American Youth Hostel	🏠		
Boundary	– – – –	Park headquarters, building	♦ ⬛
Bridge	≍	Parking (ride start)	P
Campground	▲	Parking (other)	ⓟ
Compass	⊕	Paved recreation path	～
Creek	⌒	Paved road	∿
Dirt road or trail	⌗⌗⌗	Picnic tables	⊼
Ferry	⛴	Radar dish	📡
Fort	⊥	Rock quarry	✕
Gate	•–•	Route	➤
Golf course	⚑	Route direction	▼
Heliport	🚁	Scale	▬
Hospital	✚	School	🏫
Interstate	～	Slope rating	① gradual
			② moderate
Interstate number	280		③ steep
Lake	⬭	State highway	24
Lighthouse	☼	Town, city	O
Marsh	⌄	Train tracks	+–+–+
Mountaintop	△	U.S. Highway	101
Observatory	⬛	Windmill	🗼

Bolinas Ridge

DISTANCE >>> 30 miles

TERRAIN >>> Moderately hilly

TRAFFIC >>> Bicyclists, hikers, equestrians, light to moderate car traffic

HOW TO GET THERE >>> From Highway 101 north of San Francisco, take the Highway 1 exit. Continue up a ridge and down to the coast on a winding road, passing Stinson Beach on the way. Park in or around Bolinas on a turnout.

ARGUABLY THE MOST SCENIC RIDING location in the Bay Area, Bolinas Ridge offers a bird's-eye view of Marin County at its best. Midway through the ride, you leave the redwoods and enter meadowlands, brown or green depending on the season.

The ride starts in downtown Bolinas, although you may want to park elsewhere and ride into town. This quiet rural community likes its privacy. Every time Caltrans crews erect a Bolinas road sign, it's promptly torn down.

Wildlife abounds in this lush valley formed by the San Andreas Fault. Nearby Bolinas Lagoon has some of the best bird viewing in the

Bolinas Ridge Trail overlooks Tomales Bay in the distance.

MILEAGE LOG

0.0 Start mileage at intersection of Brighton Avenue and Olema Bolinas Road, where Olema Bolinas Road becomes Wharf Road in downtown Bolinas.

0.8 Right at stop sign, staying on Olema Bolinas Road.

1.9 Right at unmarked intersection, staying on Olema Bolinas Road.

2.0 Straight at Highway 1 stop sign to Fairfax Bolinas Road, beginning 4.3-mile climb.

6.3 Left onto Bolinas Ridge Trail at gate. 9.6 McCurdy Trail on left. Goes to Highway 1; legal for bikes. 11.2 Randall Trail on left. Goes to Highway 1; legal for bikes. 12.2 Shafter Bridge Trail on right; legal for bikes. 12.6 Gate; 14.0 Gate; 14.3 Gate; 15.0 Gate.

16.0 Left at Y in trail to Sir Francis Drake Boulevard. 16.2 Gate.

17.4 Left on Sir Francis Drake Boulevard.

18.5 Left on Highway 1 at stop sign. Town of Olema.

27.6 Right on Olema Bolinas Road.

29.6 End ride in Bolinas.

Bay Area. Mature eucalyptus trees lining Olema Bolinas Road shelter migratory monarch butterflies during the winter.

After crossing Highway 1, begin a moderately steep climb on the lightly traveled Fairfax Bolinas Road. You'll see Bolinas Lagoon and the ocean below. Turn left at the summit, where there's a steel gate marking Bolinas Ridge Trail. In wet weather, tree roots make the first half-mile hazardous. The trail climbs and follows an obtrusive wire fence for a mile or so before heading into the redwoods.

It's all downhill once you're out of the redwoods. Close the gates behind you, and watch out for cattle.

Turn left on Sir Francis Drake Boulevard and zoom downhill to the town of Olema. There's a food store on the left along Highway 1. Finish the ride by continuing south on the Shoreline Highway to Bolinas. Two-lane Highway 1 has narrow shoulders and light to moderate traffic.

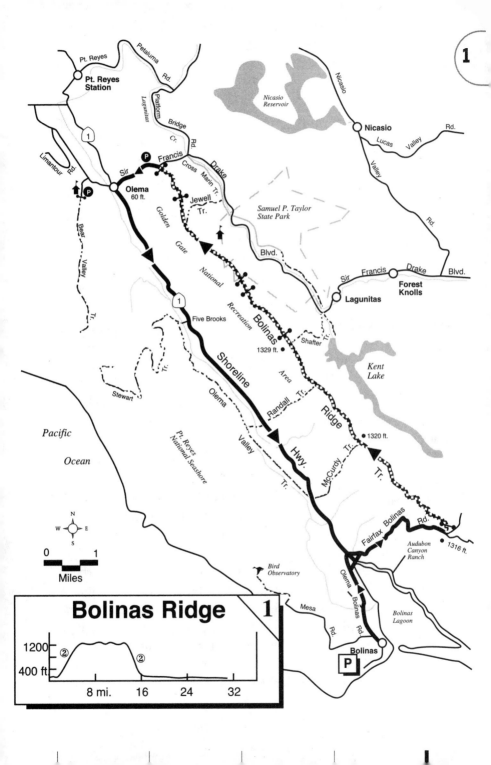

1

Pt. Reyes

Petaluma Rd.

Pt. Reyes Station

Nicasio Rd.

Nicasio Reservoir

Nicasio

Rd.

Lagunitas

Platform Bridge Rd.

Cr.

Lucas Valley Rd.

1

Sir Francis

Cross

Mann Tr.

Drake

Olema 60 ft.

Limantour Rd.

P

P

Samuel P. Taylor State Park

Jewell Tr.

Golden

Gate

National

Blvd.

Sir Francis Drake Blvd.

Lagunitas

Forest Knolls

Bear Valley Tr.

1

Recreation

Bolinas

Area

Five Brooks

1329 ft.

Shafter Tr.

Kent Lake

Shoreline

Ridge

Stewart Tr.

Olema

Randall Tr.

Hwy.

McCurdy Tr.

Tr.

1320 ft.

Pacific

Ocean

Pt. Reyes National Seashore

Valley

Tr.

Tr.

Fairfax Bolinas Rd.

Audubon Canyon Ranch

1316 ft.

N
W — E
S

0   1

Miles

Bird Observatory

Olema

Bolinas Rd.

Rd.

Bolinas Lagoon

Mesa Rd.

Bolinas

P

Bolinas Ridge

1

1200

②   ②

400 ft

8 mi.   16   24   32

② Miwok Trail

DISTANCE >>> 8 miles

TERRAIN >>> Long hills on dirt roads, with one section of wide single-track

TRAFFIC >>> Bicyclists, hikers, equestrians

HOW TO GET THERE >>> Going north on Highway 101 and the Golden Gate Bridge, take the Alexander (Sausalito) exit on your right after passing the vista point. After about two-tenths of a mile take a left at Bunker Road, which goes through a tunnel under Highway 101. Follow Bunker Road to Rodeo Lagoon, where there's plenty of parking at the long, white wooden building next to the Miwok trailhead. Heading south on Highway 101, take the Sausalito exit before reaching the Golden Gate Bridge, and go under Highway 101 downhill to Danes Drive.

WITHIN 10 MILES OF ONE OF THE most crowded cities in the country, there's a mountain bike ride with views of the Pacific Ocean, Mt. Tamalpais, and San Francisco Bay. The trip starts at sea level and climbs as high at 800 feet. The uphill stretches, on mostly smooth dirt roads, won't test your lowest gears, but they won't go unnoticed either.

Controversy continues over which trails should be available for bicycling in the Golden Gate National Recreation Area (GGNRA) in the Marin headlands, but for now you can make a nice loop from Rodeo Lagoon to Tennessee Valley and back. There's one section of wide single-track even hard-core riders can sink their knobbies into.

Begin riding from Rodeo Lagoon at the Miwok Trail entrance. In a short distance bear right onto Bobcat Trail. There's a gradual climb for a mile up treeless Gerbode Valley, surrounded by hills bristling with power lines and cellular towers. After a mile the climb steepens on the wide dirt road. Near the summit of Wolfback Ridge at 2.5 miles, you'll come to a junction with a parallel trail. Keep left and continue, with a short climb to the final summit. At the ridgetop take a breather and enjoy the view of the Pacific, sailboats on the bay, and Mt. Tamalpais.

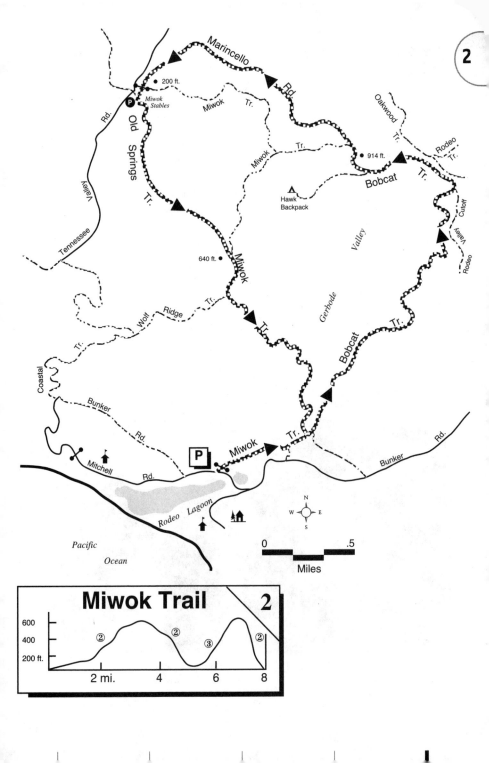

Marincello Rd.

200 ft.

Miwok Stables

Old Springs Rd.

Miwok Tr.

Oakwood Tr.

Rodeo Tr.

914 ft.

Bobcat Tr.

Tennessee Valley

Hawk Backpack

Valley

Valley Cutoff

Rodeo

Old Springs Tr.

640 ft.

Miwok Tr.

Gerbode

Wolf Ridge Tr.

Coastal Tr.

Bobcat Tr.

Bunker Rd.

Miwok Tr.

Bunker Rd.

Mitchell Rd.

P

Rodeo Lagoon

Pacific Ocean

N
W   E
S

0   .5

Miles

Miwok Trail 2

600
400
200 ft.

②   ②   ③   ②

2 mi.   4   6   8

2 MILEAGE LOG

0.0 Ride starts on Miwok (pronounced Me-walk) Trail at Rodeo Lagoon. There's a portable toilet next to the trailhead. Begin mileage at the white iron gate. 0.3 Junction on right.

0.5 Right at Y junction onto Bobcat Trail. 0.55 Keep left at junction and begin gradual climb that steepens at about one mile. 2.0 Climb eases.

2.5 Keep left at Y junction, staying on Bobcat Trail. Gradual descent followed by another short climb. 2.7 Hawk Trail to campground on left.

3.3 Right at Y junction at summit onto Marincello Trail. Begin descent to Tennessee Valley.

4.7 Left at iron gate. Walk bike through Miwok Stables to Old Springs Trail, signed on your right.

4.8 Right onto Old Springs Trail, beginning steep climb. Some walking may be required in first 100 yards. 5.5 Summit.

5.9 Right at T junction onto Miwok Trail. 6.1 Begin descent.

7.3 Keep right at junction with Bobcat Trail.

7.8 End ride at starting point.

Bobcat Trail crests an exposed ridge in the Golden Gate National Recreation Area.

Begin your descent on Marincello Trail, a wide, rutted road. Watch for equestrians, who frequently use the trail. I slow to a crawl when passing and exchange pleasantries to put the horse and rider at ease. Miwok Stables at the bottom of the hill hosts all sorts of equestrian activities. Ride around the gate and turn left to enter the stable area. Obey the signs and walk your bike a short distance to Old Springs Trail.

There's a rough, rocky outcropping that the strongest riders may be able to ride up, but mere mortals will walk for a short section. The wide, rocky single-track climbs through brush along a ridge. It's easy to see trail users descending your way. At the top of the climb you'll roll along for a few tenths of a mile before arriving at the Miwok Trail junction. Go right and shortly you'll begin a long, gradual descent on Miwok, your reward for all the climbing.

Take Miwok back to the starting point. Soil conditions and excellent drainage make the Marin Headlands a great place to ride year-round, except during periods of heavy rain.

③ Mt. Tamalpais

DISTANCE >>> 22 miles

TERRAIN >>> Hilly

TRAFFIC >>> Bicyclists, hikers, light car traffic

HOW TO GET THERE >>> From Highway 101 north out of San Francisco, take the Highway 1 exit, following the Sausalito Bridgeway exit, just before the Richardson Bay Bridge. Coming from the north take the Highway 1 exit, turn right and right again to drive under Highway 101.

AS YOU RIDE ON THE OLD RAILROAD grade up Mt. Tamalpais, you'll understand why the modern mountain bike was invented here. Creators Joe Breeze, Gary Fisher, Charlie Kelly, and Otis Guy lived at the base of the mountain when they started riding one-speed clunkers, first downhill and later in both directions after gears were added. Within a decade, the mountain bike had progressed from a one-speed bomber to a technologically sophisticated multigeared wonder. Joe Breeze built the first modern mountain bike in 1977.

This tour starts in Marin City under a bridge that is part of Highway 101. You'll ride north through Mill Valley, pick up the railroad grade to

Coyote Ridge Trail climbs steeply from Muir Beach.

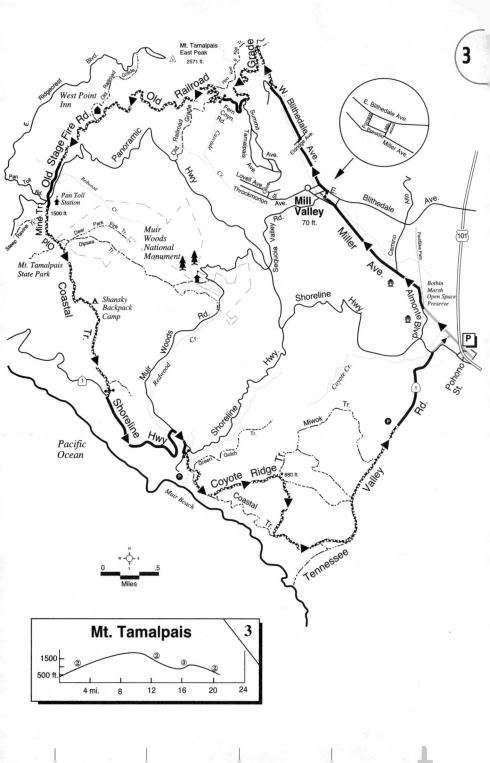

Mt. Tamalpais
East Peak
2571 ft.

Ridgecrest   Blvd.

E.

West Point
Inn

Old   Railroad   Grade

W. Blithedale Ave.

E. Blithedale Ave.

Frustal
Presidio
Elwood

Miller Ave.

Panoramic

Old Stage Fire Rd.

Old   Railroad   Grade

Hoo Koo E Koo Tr.

Summit

Tamalpais   Ave.

Fern
Cnyn.
Rd.

Cascade

Cr.

Lovell Ave.

Throckmorton   Ave.

Eldridge Ave.

Blithedale   Ave.

Alto

101

Mill
Valley
70 ft.

Pan
Toll
Rd.

Redwood

Mine Tr.

Pan Toll
Station
1500 ft.

Cr.

Deer   Park   Fire   Tr.

Dipsea

Tr.

Muir Woods
National
Monument

Sequoia   Valley   Rd.

Miller   Ave.

Camino

Almonte Blvd.

PacBike Path

Bothin
Marsh
Open Space
Preserve

P

Mt. Tamalpais
State Park

Coastal   Tr.

Pio

Shansky
Backpack
Camp

Muir   Woods   Rd.

Redwood   Cr.

Shoreline   Hwy.

Shoreline   Hwy.

Coyote Cr.

1

Pohono
St.

P

1

Steep Ravine

Shoreline   Hwy.

Pacific
Ocean

Green   Gulch

Coyote   Ridge   Tr.

880 ft.

Miwok   Tr.

Tr.

P

Valley   Rd.

Muir Beach

Coastal   Tr.

Tennessee   Valley

0   .5

Miles

N
W   E
S

Mt. Tamalpais   3

1500 ft.
500 ft.

②   ②   ③   ②

4 mi.   8   12   16   20   24

3 West Point, head to the ocean, and return on Highway 1 by Tennessee Valley in the Golden Gate National Recreation Area.

Hikers and bicyclists enjoy using the railroad grade year-round. The speed limit is 15 mph, 5 mph when passing other trail users. Many trails and roads connect with the railroad grade, which snakes its way up the mountain in 281 curves.

All that remains of the railroad is a concrete platform, once called Mesa Junction Station, 6.5 miles into the ride at the junction to Muir Woods. Farther up, there was a water tower; you can still get a drink from its source at Fern Canyon Falls.

West Point Inn, established in 1904, lies at an important trail junction. (It's about a mile and a half from here to the summit, where there's a concession stand.) Keep left at West Point and go to Pan Toll Station to pick up the Coastal Fire Trail. The trail descends to Highway 1 and gives you a view of the rocky Pacific coast. Go left on Highway 1 and descend to Redwood Creek and the Pelican Inn, a restaurant-bar modeled after an English pub. It's a steep climb from Muir Beach to Coyote Ridge. At the ridge trail junction, go right and descend to Tennessee Valley Road on a wide fire road. You'll enjoy a flat ride through the valley to Highway 1.

MILEAGE LOG

0.0 Start mileage directly under Richardson Bay Bridge, Highway 101. Parking is available next to the bridge off Pohono Street. Ride north on recreation path. Sections of path may flood at high tide. 0.1 Cross bridge over Coyote Creek inlet.

0.5 Left at crosswalk, then immediate right onto Miller Avenue in bike lane. 1.1 Camino Alto traffic light. Tamalpais High School on left.

2.1 Right on Millwood at green bike route sign, followed by immediate left on Presidio Avenue. Right on Forrest.

2.3 Left on East Blithedale Avenue at stop sign.

2.5 Straight on West Blithedale Avenue.

2.8 Keep left.

3.6 Right at Blithedale Summit Gate, beginning Old Railroad Grade.

3.8 Straight at junction.

4.4 Left at junction, downhill. Former site of Horseshoe Bend Trestle. 5.1 McKinley Cut. Rock was blasted to lay track. Named for President McKinley, who visited this site.

5.6 Right on Fern Canyon Road at top of Summit Avenue, paved. 6.2 Pavement ends; railroad grade continues at gate.

6.5 Right at junction, then immediate right again. Remains of railroad platform on left.

6.9 Left at junction with Hoo-Koo-E-Koo Trail (second bend of Double Bow Knot). 8.0 Fern Canyon Falls. Train water tower was located here.

8.8 West Point Inn. Left to Old Stage Road. To reach Mt. Tam summit, go right. Drinking fountain at junction. 10.4 Pavement. Continue straight. Drinking fountain.

10.9 Cross Panoramic Highway to Pan Toll park headquarters and parking area. Drinking fountain and rest-rooms. Continue west on paved road. 11.2 Maintenance station. Begin Old Mine Road, dirt.

11.4 Keep right. Deer Park Fire Road junction on left.

11.5 Keep right at junction.

12.5 Keep right at junction. 12.8 Shansky Backpack Camp on left. 13.5 Steel gate and flower garden both sides of trail. Continue straight. Do not disturb flowers.

13.7 Right at two round wood posts with gap in fence to Coast Highway. Descend past Muir Beach Overlook on right. 15.2 Muir Woods Road on left.

15.4 Right at Pacific Way. Pelican Inn on corner.

15.6 Left at aluminum gate next to bridge over creek.

15.9 Left at Muir Beach Lagoon junction. Right at next junction up steep hill on dirt road, 200 yards from gate. (Left goes to Green Gulch Farm and Zen Center.) 16.4 Coastal Trail on right.

16.7 Right at gate and continue straight up steep hill.

17.2 Right at junction on top of Coyote Ridge. Right again in 100 yards on dirt road. 18.6 Coastal Trail on right.

19.2 Left at bottom of hill in Tennessee Valley. Pavement begins in 0.3 miles. 19.9 Miwok Stables and parking lot.

21.5 Left under bridge at Highway 1 and Tennessee Valley Road junction. At gravel parking lot on left, take trail under bridge (floods at high tide), which becomes paved recreation path back to start of ride.

21.7 Left at first junction and then right on recreation path that returns to starting point.

21.8 End ride.

3

3

Mt. Tam's gently sloped railroad grade invites family riding.

The Mill Valley & Mount Tamalpais Railway Company, founded by Sidney Cushing in 1896, built the railroad after overcoming objections and lawsuits by Mill Valley residents, who didn't like having their quiet streets ripped up for the railway. Shay locomotives hauled tourists to an elegant summit hotel.

The railroad became a popular tourist attraction but hardly a financial success. It weathered lean years and even extended its line to Muir Woods with gravity cars. However, automobiles, buses, and the Great Depression spelled doom for the railroad. Ridgecrest Boulevard to the Mt. Tamalpais summit was completed in 1924, giving people easy access. The railroad shut down for good in 1929 after a fire swept across the mountain, destroying the hotel and a locomotive. A year later the rails were removed and the right-of-way turned over to hikers.

Repack Road

DISTANCE >>> 10 miles

TERRAIN >>> Mostly continuous climbing for 6 miles, followed by a steep descent

TRAFFIC >>> Bicyclists, hikers, equestrians, light car traffic

HOW TO GET THERE >>> Leaving San Francisco from Highway 101 north, take the exit for Sir Francis Drake Boulevard (San Anselmo) going west. Drive about 6 miles on a mostly two-lane road to downtown Fairfax. At the traffic light next to the tall, blocky Fairfax Theater sign, turn left and then take another immediate left onto Broadway. Go about 100 yards and turn right onto Bolinas Avenue. Stay on Bolinas for about a mile and turn left at a green sign indicating Deer Park Picnic Grounds, which will put you on Porteous Avenue. Go about a half-mile to the end of the road, Deer Park. There's parking for about 25 cars.

WHEN MOUNTAIN BIKING BLOSsomed in the late 1970s, Repack Road became one of the bestknown descents. Like a famous ski run, it still draws mountain bikers from miles around.

Races took place at Repack starting in 1976, an event that galvanized mountain bike riders to improve their mounts. It was the buzz about Repack racing that launched mountain biking as an international sport. This location is the Mt. Sinai of mountain biking, and the Marin Municipal Water District (MMWD) is mountain bike Mecca. When mountain bikers commemorated the twentieth anniversary of the Repack races in 1996, Joe Breeze, who built the first modern mountain bike, read a eulogy.

Repack Road isn't much to see, but the visuals aren't why Repack became famous. Repack overlooks Fairfax, home to some of the first mountain bikers. There are miles of open space and trails surrounding the wooded community, and the town's narrow streets with no parked cars make bicycling more appealing.

The ride begins at Deer Park, one of the few locations in Fairfax with public parking. Starting from the outer parking lot, ride to the left of Deer Park Elementary School on a trail, cross a soccer field,

MILEAGE LOG

4

0.0 Start mileage at the wood-carved Deer Park sign at the park entrance. Ride on the paved road to Deer Park Elementary School, keeping left. Restrooms on left. 0.1 Take narrow trail immediately left of the school building. Ride across a soccer field behind school. Trail heads toward iron gate marking the beginning of Deer Park Road. 0.2 Ride around gate and continue on fire road with creek on right. 0.5 Begin climbing.

0.9 Keep left at four-way intersection, continuing climb. 1.3 Take second fire road from right at five-corners intersection, continuing climb. 1.6 Road levels and begins short descent.

1.9 Right on paved Sky Oaks Road.

2.2 Left at fire road gate. Unpaved parking area located just beyond gate.

2.3 Right at Y junction.

2.5 Right at T junction. Meadow Country Club Golf Course on left. 3.0 Paved parking lot. Go straight through parking lot to Bolinas Road.

3.1 Left on Bolinas Road.

4.3 Right on unpaved Pine Mountain Road at gate. Parking area across road.

5.3 Keep right at Oat Hill Road junction.

5.8 Keep right. Becomes San Geronimo Ridge Road.

6.2 Right at junction onto unmarked Repack Road. 6.3 Gate.

7.9 Right over bridge crossing creek. Stay on the main dirt road, which has a brief climb followed by a downhill. 8.1 Ford creek. 8.2 Ford creek. 8.21 Ford creek. 8.3 Ford creek. 8.34 Gate at Elliott Preserve entrance. Begin paved Cascade Drive. Follow Cascade Drive downhill.

9.7 Right on Bolinas Avenue at stop sign.

9.74 Left at green Deer Park Picnic Ground sign, Porteous Avenue.

10.1 End ride at Deer Park.

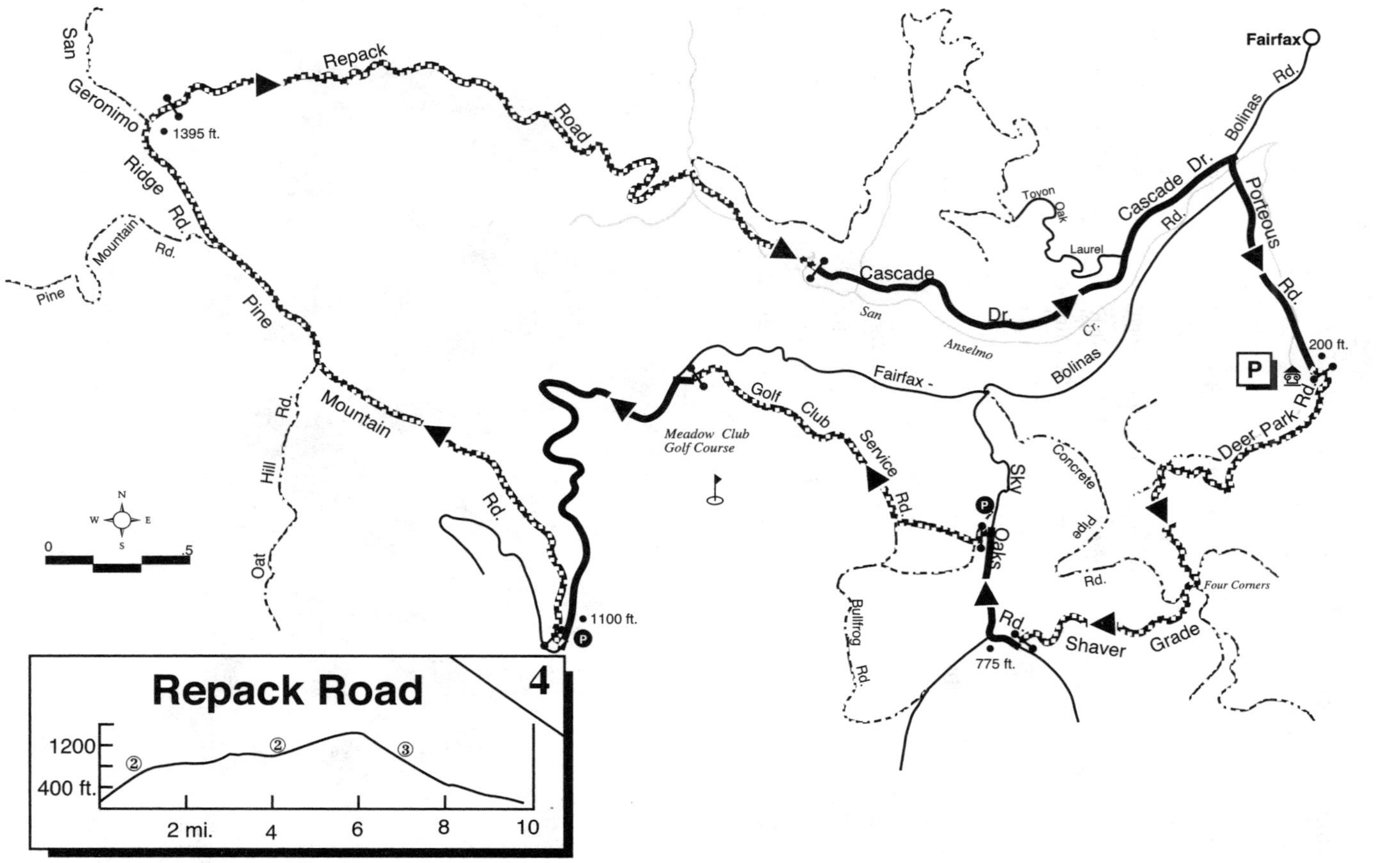

Fairfax

Bolinas Rd.

Porteous Rd.

200 ft.

Deer Park Rd.

P

Cascade Dr.

Laurel

Oak

Toyon

Cascade Dr.

Bolinas

San Anselmo

Fairfax -

Concrete Pipe

Rd.

Four Corners

Shaver Grade

Sky Oaks Rd.

775 ft.

Golf Club

Service Rd.

Bullfrog Rd.

Meadow Club
Golf Course

Road

Repack

Mountain Rd.

1100 ft.

P

Oat Hill Rd.

Pine

1395 ft.

San Geronimo Ridge Rd.

Mountain Rd.

Pine

N
W   E
S

0   5

Repack Road

4

1200
400 ft.

2 mi.   4   6   8   10

② ② ③

4 and take Deer Park Fire Road. The MMWD restricts bike riding to fire roads.

You'll follow a stream for a short distance before starting a continuous climb through the oak-covered hills. The fairly steep climb will give your knobbies a workout.

There will be two major junctions before you reach paved Sky Oaks Road, which takes you downhill to a parking lot. From here it's a gentle climb around the edge of Meadow Country Club Golf Course. Watch for wild turkeys in this area. You'll probably hear them before seeing them.

Fairfax-Bolinas Road continues the climb to Pine Mountain Road. Turn right onto unpaved Pine Mountain Road; here's where the real climbing begins. The road gives mountain bikers a chance to test their riding skills. I rode here in 1982 and 1984 when the road wasn't as rocky. Over the years the topsoil has washed away, leaving nothing but large rocks and boulders. Today's suspension bikes will help smooth out the bumps.

The water district's pristine beauty is much in evidence on Pine Mountain Road, a high-alpine setting distinguished by stubby

A pair of wild turkeys cross the road bordering the Meadow Country Club Golf Course.

You'll "rock and roll" on San Geronimo Road.

cedar trees and close-cropped grasses. It's easy to forget you're only a few miles from the congested Bay Area.

Just as the trail levels out following an extremely rocky section on San Geronimo Ridge, you'll come to an unmarked intersection, Repack Road. A wood trail sign has been removed. Repack Road takes off to your right, climbing briefly before plunging down the mountain. Rocky at first, the fire road gradually smooths out, but watch out for water-carved ruts along the way.

The 1.8-mile descent ends at San Anselmo Creek and a bridge. Cross the bridge and continue on a narrow trail, fording Cascade Creek, a tributary of San Anselmo Creek, four times. The creek is usually dry. Exit Elliott Nature Preserve onto Cascade Drive and take the quiet residential street downhill to Bolinas Road. Return to Deer Park.

MMWD lands are closed to the public during times of high fire danger. Be sure to check with district officials during hot, dry spells.

5 Briones Park

DISTANCE >>> 15 miles

TERRAIN >>> Hilly and steep in spots

TRAFFIC >>> Bicyclists, hikers, equestrians

HOW TO GET THERE >>> From Highway 24 in Orinda, take the Moraga Way/Camino Pablo exit in Orinda. Go north on Camino Pablo, then right on Bear Creek Road after 2.5 miles. Continue 6.8 miles on Bear Creek Road to the Briones Road park entrance on the right.

BRIONES REGIONAL PARK, AN ISLAND of open space surrounded by country estates and ranches, gives the East Bay mountain biker plenty of excitement close to home. Almost all the old ranch roads winding through the park, shown as hiking trails on park maps, are open for bicycling. Volunteer trail work and participation in park meetings by the Coast Range Riders has helped keep the park open to cyclists.

In the spring, on secluded hilltops, there's a hint of the green hills of Ireland. The park has enough variety—wide valleys, high ridges, and deep canyons—to make mountain biking fun for riders of all abilities.

This hilly ride is one of many options for covering all corners of the park's 5,000 acres. Several "walls" require a dismount, even by "mountain goat riders" with extra-low gears.

Most trails are marked at intersections, but with so many junctions, it's easy to miss a turn. Trails vary from wide dirt roads to grassy paths. In the spring, cattle grazing the park can turn some trail sections into quagmires. Sometimes it's hard to tell the cattle paths from the trails.

Begin riding from the Bear Creek Road staging area, where there's a drinking fountain and restroom. Ride north from the parking lot on Abrigo Valley Trail and begin a steady climb through a wooded canyon with a stream. The road takes you to a valley and lush meadow with a picnic area at Wee-Ta-Chi Camp, a tranquil setting protected by giant bay trees.

Briones Crest Trail overlooks the park.

The trail turns narrow and steep beyond the camp. After a hairpin turn, you'll come to a ridge with a grand view of Mt. Diablo, Benicia-Martinez Bridge, Mt. Tamalpais, and Mt. St. Helena to the north.

As you descend Briones Crest Trail, you'll see two small ponds. Sindicich Lagoon on Lagoon Trail is fenced to keep out cattle. There's a long, bumpy descent on Toyon Canyon Trail and Pine Tree Trail, named for the trees growing here. Orchard Trail is the site of a former orchard and ranch. Coulter pine, with their huge cones more than a foot long and weighing two pounds, grow near the orchard.

Cross the paved Old Briones Road and descend to a wide valley, where you'll find the Alhambra Creek Valley Staging Area. Follow Alhambra Creek Trail up a valley cloaked in blue lupine in the spring. You'll have a steady climb through oaks and bay laurels. On Spengler Trail you'll climb through a beautiful stand of oaks. After a descent, climb the first wall, about 200 yards long. Turn left and stay on Spengler Trail. You'll see ranch houses in the canyon below. Drop into a gully and assault the next wall to a ridge, where there's more climbing.

Take a hard right at a gate to join Table Top Trail. After a roller-coaster hill, you'll pass a communications tower. In the spring you'll

5 MILEAGE LOG

0.0 Start mileage at the Bear Creek entrance to Briones Regional Park off Bear Creek Road. The parking lot is about a half-mile from Bear Creek Road. Ride north on Abrigo Valley Trail.

0.9 Left at junction with Mott Peak Trail. 1.4 Maud Walen Camp on right.

1.9 Right on Briones Crest Trail.

2.2 Right at Lagoon Trail junction, staying on Briones Crest Trail.

3.0 Left on Lagoon Trail.

3.6 Right on Toyon Canyon Trail.

4.6 Left on Pine Tree Trail.

4.7 Right on Orchard Trail. 5.3 Cross Old Briones Road at Rancho Briones.

5.9 Right on Alhambra Creek Trail at Alhambra Creek Valley Staging Area. Drinking fountain and restrooms.

6.9 Left onto Spengler Trail.

7.9 Keep right at junction with Blue Oak Trail.

8.7 Left at junction, staying on Spengler Trail.

10.0 Right onto Spengler Trail. Dirt road goes to service area.

10.4 Right on Table Top Trail.

11.1 Left on Briones Crest Trail.

12.0 Right at junction.

12.1 Left on Briones Crest Trail.

12.6 Left on Mott Peak Trail.

13.0 Left on Black Oak Trail.

14.0 Right on Old Briones Road.

14.8 End ride at Bear Creek parking lot.

---

find a meadow thick with poppies. To the right, there's a panorama of Suisun Bay, and on a clear day you can see the Sierra. Most of the climbing is over now. Table Top intersects Briones Crest Trail. Ride down to Lagoon Trail, climb the hill you rode down earlier, and take a left onto Mott Peak Trail, which runs along a narrow ridge and over Mott Peak at 1,424 feet. Descend Black Oak Trail and hold onto your helmet for a steep, bumpy descent to Old Briones Road. Turn right and ride back to the Bear Creek Staging Area.

Briones Regional Park opened in 1967. Prior to its becoming a park, ranchers used the land for grazing cattle. It was left undeveloped as the San Pablo Dam watershed. The earliest settler, Felipe Briones, built a home in 1829 near the Bear Creek entrance. His land occupied part of the huge Rancho Boca de la Cañada del Pinole Mexican land grant. During Prohibition, the East Bay's isolated ranchlands became bootlegging hideouts.

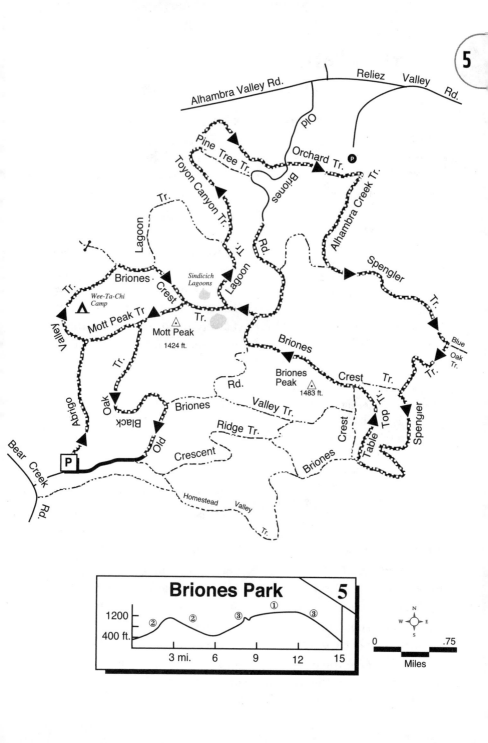

Alhambra Valley Rd.

Reliez Valley Rd.

Pine Tree Tr.

Orchard Tr. **P**

Old

Briones

Toyon Canyon Tr.

Alhambra Creek Tr.

Tr.

Lagoon

Lagoon

Spengler

Tr.

Briones

Sindicich
Lagoons

Crest

Wee-Ta-Chi
Camp

Tr.

Mott Peak Tr

Mott Peak
1424 ft.

Tr.

Tr.

Blue
Oak
Tr.

Briones

Valley

Tr.

Briones
Peak
1483 ft.

Crest

Tr.

Spengler

Oak

Tr.

Briones

Black

Old

Rd.

Valley Tr.

Table Top

Spengler

Tr.

Abrigo

Bear Creek

P

Crescent

Ridge Tr.

Briones

Crest

Rd.

Homestead Valley

Tr.

Briones Park

5

1200

400 ft.

②

②

③

①

③

3 mi.   6   9   12   15

N
W   E
S

0   .75

Miles

6 Redwood Park

DISTANCE >>> 12 miles

TERRAIN >>> One steep mile-long climb; rolling hills

TRAFFIC >>> Bicyclists, hikers, equestrians

HOW TO GET THERE >>> From Highway 580, exit at Warren Freeway (Highway 13), going north. Take the first exit, Carson Street/Redwood Road. Continue north another quarter-mile after the Carson Street stop sign, turning right onto Redwood Road. Take Redwood Road uphill for about a mile to Skyline Boulevard. Stay in the middle lane at the intersection to continue straight and then downhill. Go another 2 miles or so downhill, past the main entrance to Redwood Park, and in a short distance turn left up Pinehurst Road. Go about a mile uphill and look for the Pinehurst Gate Staging Area on the left, a dirt parking lot with no facilities. Parking at the main entrance costs $3.

IN THE EARLY 1800s, SAILORS entering San Francisco Bay used the tall redwoods as navigational landmarks. The original redwoods in Redwood Regional Park were cut down in the mid-1800s, but on this trip you'll ride through a 150-year-old redwood grove spawned from the original trees.

This urban park, overlooking Oakland, gives local riders a quick getaway. Riding clockwise around the perimeter offers vistas of the park's wooded interior, San Francisco Bay, and East Bay reservoirs.

Start the ride at Pinehurst Staging Area, overlooking Upper San Leandro Reservoir. There's a short, steep climb before the fire road levels, with a view of Moraga Valley to the east. Single-track riding is prohibited in the park.

In less than a mile you'll turn left and head down the steep Canyon Trail into Owl Canyon. At the bottom, go left at the Y junction facing a picnic area and in a short distance you'll reach a gate. Ride around the gate and through a paved parking lot to continue on the main entrance road for about 200 yards. Look for a small clearing on your right. There's a footpath down to the open area, where you'll see a kiosk and a stone monument. The historical landmark commemorates the naming of the rainbow trout species taken from San Leandro Creek in 1855.

Dunn Trail at the Graham Trail junction passes a Douglas fir grove.

Cross the stone-lined creek and immediately go right on Bridle Trail. In a short distance you'll make a U-turn and begin a steep 1-mile climb through an oak-covered hillside to about 1,200 feet. If you can ride all the way, without walking some of the distance, enter the next mountain bike race. You'll be a contender.

Once the climb levels out, the rest of the ride offers short, fun ups and downs. All junctions are marked, but sometimes the wooden posts are hidden behind bushes. Bring a map.

On West Ridge Trail be sure to make the left turn onto Dunn Trail, which has a gentle descent through redwoods and Douglas fir. At the western end of the trail you'll break out into the open and enjoy views of San Francisco Bay.

Leave Dunn Trail at mile 4.9 and begin a short, steep climb on Graham Trail. After leveling out, the trail narrows, offering views of the park's woodlands. The trail winds through dense groves of redwoods from here to the Skyline Gate Staging Area. There's a fair amount of bicycle and foot traffic, so keep your speed down.

East Ridge Trail, one of the most popular staging areas in the park, has lots of hikers. The trail is wide for the first mile, so there's plenty of

6 MILEAGE LOG

0.0 Start mileage at iron gate, beginning 0.2-mile climb.

0.9 Left on Canyon Road and begin descent.

1.3 Left at Y junction (restrooms are located to the right a short distance). 1.34 Go around iron gate and continue on paved road through parking lot. Keep left on main entrance road.

1.7 Right at narrow path to small open area and trailhead. Look for a white sign with a bicycle and two arrows. Historical marker. Cross creek and turn right onto Bridle Trail.

1.8 Left, U-turn onto West Ridge Trail. Begin steep 1-mile climb.

3.4 Left on Baccharis Trail at Y junction.

3.8 Left at Y junction onto Dunn Trail.

4.0 Keep right on Dunn Trail at junction with Monteiro Trail.

5.0 Keep right onto Graham Trail at T junction. 5.7 Keep right at junction with Roberts Trail.

6.0 Keep right at second Roberts Trail junction.

6.15 Left onto West Ridge Trail at Redwood Bowl meadow.

6.2 Keep right on West Ridge Trail.

6.3 Keep straight on West Ridge Trail at yellow signs. 6.4 Ride around iron gate, cross paved road to Chabot Space and Science Center, and pick up trail across the street. 6.7 Cross Chabot Space and Science Center parking driveway. 7.0 Moon Gate Staging Area on left. 8.2 Skyline Staging Area, paved parking lot. Restrooms, phones, water. Cross paved path and continue on East Ridge Trail. 9.0 Scenic view.

11.3 Keep straight at Canyon Trail junction on right. Begin descent.

12.2 End ride at Parkhurst Staging Area.

---

room for passing. Towering pines line East Ridge Trail, creating a natural cathedral overhead as the trail rolls along like a roller coaster. The best views of the park's interior canyon come on this wide fire road.

Watch out for cottontail rabbits and deer along the trails in the park. They're everywhere. On foggy mornings you may also see giant yellow banana slugs that live in the redwood groves.

Redwood Park is an excellent place to ride if you're new to mountain biking. The trails are smooth and not too steep, except for that 1-mile climb through the oaks.

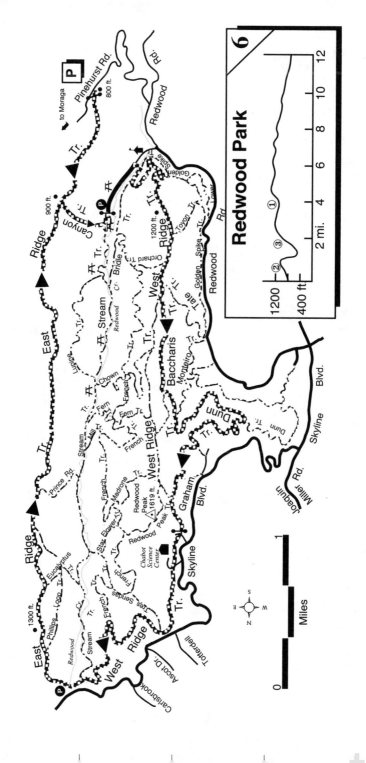

Redwood Park

6

7 Shell Ridge

AT THE WESTERN APPROACH TO Mt. Diablo there's plenty of open space for mountain bike riding, and it can be a "moo-ving" experience as you pass range cattle basking in the sun. On this loop you'll ride through open space administered by a bewildering array of organizations: the city of Walnut Creek, East Bay Municipal Utility District, the State of California, and East Bay Regional Open Space District. You'll pass through ten gates—don't forget to close them behind you.

Start riding from the end of Marshall Drive, where you'll pick up the Briones–Mt. Diablo Trail behind a fence in Shell Ridge Open Space. On this ride your orienteering skills will be put to the test. Closely track mileage, because the open space is laced with ranch roads and trails, many of them unmarked. Basically, you want to head south for almost 6 miles.

You'll begin climbing right away on a road that winds its way along the lower section of Shell Ridge, followed by the sort of rolling descents and climbs you'll encounter repeatedly throughout the ride. Be sure to conserve energy on the climbs to avoid "rolling blackouts."

Indian Creek meanders on your right. Mt. Diablo will be hidden from view until several miles into the ride. At 2.8 miles you'll break out into the open in a shallow valley with panoramic views of rolling, oak-covered hills. Equestrians frequent these open spaces regularly. Always

Mt. Diablo Summit

Stage Rd.

Wall Point Rd.

Little Pine Creek Rd.

Sunset Tr.

600 ft.
Pine Pond

North Gate Rd.

Stage Rd.

800 ft.

Stage Rd.

Macedo Ranch Staging Area P

Diablo Foothills Regional Park
Castle Rock Recreation Area P

Flood Control Dry Dam

Stage Rd.

Castle Rock Tr.

Shell Ridge Tr.

Pine Tr.

Hanging Valley Tr.

Diablo Tr.

Shell Ridge Tr.

Stonegate

Castle Rock Rd.

Borges Ranch Rd.

Borges Ranch

Diablo Tr.

Twin Ponds

Water Tank

Foothills Tr.

Costanoan

Castle Rock Rd.

300 ft.

Hanna Grove Tr.

Costanoan Tr.

Top Tr.

Table Tr.

Foggy Knob Tr.

Top Tr.

Ridge Tr.

Costanoan Tr.

Mt. Diablo Tr.

Briones-Mt. Diablo Tr.

Shell Ridge Tr.

Rockspring Pl.

Walnut Blvd.

Lower Buck Tr.

Upper Buck Tr.

Deer Lake

800 ft.

Briones-Mt. Diablo Tr.

Top Tr.

Hammill Tr.

Briones-Mt. Diablo Tr.

Top Ridge

Indian Creek Tr.

La Casa Via

Marshall Dr.

300 ft.

P

Lime Oak Tr.

Fossil Hill Tr.

N
W E
S

Miles

0   1

Shell Ridge

900

300 ft.

① ②   ②   ②   ②   ②

3mi   6   9   12

7

MILEAGE LOG

0.0 Start mileage at trailhead next to large wooden sign. Go right on dirt road, Briones–Mt. Diablo Trail.

0.1 Left at Y junction next to fence.

0.3 Left at Y junction.

0.5 Keep straight at T junction on right. 0.9 Indian Creek Trail on right.

1.1 Keep right at Ginder Gap Trail junction on left.

1.2 Keep straight, at trail junction to your right.

1.24 Right on Briones–Mt. Diablo Trail.

1.5 Keep straight, small trail to right. 1.7 Gate, start climb.

2.1 Keep straight at Sugarloaf Shell Ridge Trail on right.

2.6 Keep straight at Twin Ponds Trail on right. Continue straight for about 50 yards and go through another gate. Twin Ponds Trail continues to the left at this junction.

2.8 Keep right at Y junction after going through gate.

3.18 Keep straight at T junction on left.

3.2 Keep left at Y junction. 3.5 Pond on right.

4.1 Keep straight at T junction on right.

4.3 Keep straight. Gate.

4.8 Keep left at junction with single-track on right. No cheating!

5.3 Left at signed Y junction. Right goes to Macedo Ranch Staging Area in 0.3 miles. Start climb for about 0.3 miles.

5.8 Left at Y junction on Stage Road. Begin half-mile descent. Wall Point Trail to right goes up steeply.

6.3 Left at T junction continuing on Stage Road.

6.7 Keep straight at Burma Road junction on right. 6.8 Water hole. 6.85 Ford creek. 6.93 Ford creek. 6.96 Ford creek. 7.1 Ford creek. 7.2 Ford creek. 7.3 Ford creek. 7.7 Gate. 7.8 Ford creek. 7.83 Ford creek. 7.9 Ford creek. 8.0 Ford creek.

8.2 Keep left at Y junction. Trail on right crosses creek. 8.3 Old dam spillway on right.

8.4 Keep right at junction, continuing downhill.

8.5 Go through gate, keeping right at Y junction, and continue on dirt road.

8.53 Keep left at junction. 8.6 Castle Rock Park sign. Restrooms and water in park. 8.8 begin paved road. 9.0 Ride around closed gate. Trail access on left. Parking available. Continue out of park on paved road. 9.8 Old Borges Ranch access road on left.

10.2 Left on Comistas Drive.

About four miles into the ride, Briones–Mt. Diablo Trail rolls over oak-covered hills.

10.2 Left on paved Hanna Grove Trail (Castle Rock Road). Look for a large, bright-green sign with white lettering. Begin climb on Hanna Grove Trail. Costanoan Trail goes off to right. 10.5 Begin dirt road at green iron gate. Keep straight on other side of gate.

11.0 Keep left at Y junction with signed Flat Top Trail.

11.4 Right at T junction onto Costanoan Trail. Begin steep climb.

11.8 Keep straight at T junction with Flat Top Trail on right.

12.3 Keep straight on Costanoan Trail at T junction with Ginder Gap Trail on left.

12.4 Left at Y junction onto Hammill Trail. 12.47 Go through gate. 12.5 Right at Y junction.

12.5 Keep left at Y junction with Upper Buck Trail.

12.9 Keep left at junction. 12.9 Go through gate. 13.4 Cross paved road and pick up trail straight ahead. Ride down narrow trail to pick up main trail or go right 10 yards and turn left onto trail.

13.7 End ride at Indian Valley School.

7 be on the lookout for riders, and no "horsing" around. Cattle live here as well. They're harmless if left alone.

At nearly 6 miles you'll turn east onto Stage Road, descending a steep hill with numerous sandstone shelfs. You're entering Pine Canyon, a heavily wooded area that has a riparian habitat at the bottom thanks to Pine Creek, sheltered by willow, oaks, elderberry, sycamore, and cottonwoods.

Now the fun begins. You'll ford Pine Creek ten times in the next mile and a half on a gentle descent. If you don't know how to ride through creeks, you should have learned by the tenth crossing.

You'll reach pavement at Castle Rock Park and stay on pavement for another 1.6 miles. Find Hanna Grove Trail, which turns off a suburban street, and begin climbing. You'll continue climbing for almost 2 miles, with one fairly steep section overlooking Borges Ranch. After the climb there's a steep, bumpy descent followed by another climb to Hammill Trail. From here it's mostly downhill back to where you started.

Some of the credit for open space around Mt. Diablo goes to an organization called Save Mount Diablo, established in December 1971. Its continuing goal is to protect and preserve Mt. Diablo, primarily by pushing for legislative attention and state park bond acts.

Alpine Road

DISTANCE >>> 14 miles

TERRAIN >>> Long hills, steep descent

TRAFFIC >>> Bicyclists, hikers, equestrians, light car traffic

HOW TO GET THERE >>> Take the Sand Hill Road exit off Interstate 280 and go west for about 5 miles. Turn right about a half-mile past the Portola Valley Town Center Shopping Center into the Spring Ridge MROSD parking lot. It's right before a sweeping left turn with a white guard rail.

ALPINE ROAD IS A "MOUNTAIN BIKE boulevard" to Midpeninsula riders, due to its proximity to Palo Alto and relatively easy grade to Skyline Boulevard. Over the years, the road's condition has varied from excellent to impassible. Heavy rains in the mid-1980s caused a landslide near the start of the dirt road, dissuading most cyclists from using the route. Local cyclists built a narrow trail through the slide, and further improved the road by cleaning culverts and filling ruts. In the winter of 1989, San Mateo County graded the road, uncovering a long-forgotten bridge over Corte Madera Creek. In 2001, upper Alpine Road was more trail than road.

In 1995, a section of road slid away, leaving a cliff. San Mateo County, which maintains the road, has no plans to repair it. Cyclists must take a steep trail to navigate around the slide. In contrast, the town of Portola Valley somehow found a lot of government dollars to repave and improve the lower, little-used section of Alpine Road in 2000.

While San Mateo County still maintains the right-of-way, the Midpeninsula Regional Open Space District (MROSD) owns most of the land around the road. The road was closed to car traffic in the late 1960s.

Start riding from the Spring Ridge Midpeninsula Regional Open Space parking lot on Portola Valley Road, about a half-mile south of the Portola Valley at Town Center Shopping Center. Ride south on Portola Road, and take the first right onto Willowbrook Drive, a quiet rural

MILEAGE LOG

0.0 Start mileage on Portola Road at the MROSD Spring Ridge entrance.

0.1 Right on Willowbrook Drive.

1.0 Right on Alpine Road at stop sign.

3.1 Keep right at junction with Joaquin Road. 3.4 Green gate. Ride around gate on right and the dirt begins. 3.5 Corte Madera Creek bridge. 3.9 Mud Turn, muddy when wet. 4.0 Spur trail on right.

4.1 Right on bypass trail around road slide a short distance ahead.

4.4 Right back on Alpine Road, continuing climb. 4.5 Crazy Pete's Road on right. 4.7 Trail on right. 5.3 Meadow Trail on right.

5.7 Right on Page Mill Road at gate, beginning pavement.

6.3 Right on Skyline Boulevard at stop sign, continuing climb.

7.4 Overlook. Begin 1.6-mile descent. 8.1 Crazy Pete's Road on right. 9.0 Fogerty Winery. 11.2 Windy Hill parking, restrooms.

11.6 Right on Spring Ridge Road at gate. Begin descending wide trail on left. 13.0 Closed trail on right. 13.4 Sausal Trail on left.

13.5 Left at T junction.

14.0 Right on narrow trail to Spring Ridge parking lot. Spring Ridge Road ends here. Gate straight ahead.

14.1 End ride at parking lot.

---

street that bridges to Alpine Road. The narrow Alpine Road winds through a beautiful tree-covered canyon, following Corte Madera Creek for 2 miles. The road turns to dirt at a green gate next to a private driveway. It climbs steadily, a pleasant contrast to the steep Page Mill Road. The trail offers spectacular views of Santa Clara Valley at its upper reaches. But beware, the road turns to sticky mud in rain.

You'll encounter a barricade where the bypass trail begins. It's a tough climb on the single-track trail, but with a lot of muscle and the right gears, stronger riders can clear it.

At Page Mill Road go right and continue to Skyline Boulevard, where you'll turn right and begin a nice descent after a little more climbing. At the Windy Hill parking area you'll have a rare opportunity to see both the Pacific Ocean and Santa Clara Valley by looking left and then right. A short distance from the Windy Hill parking lot, turn right onto Spring Ridge Road. It's mostly downhill on the trail, which has

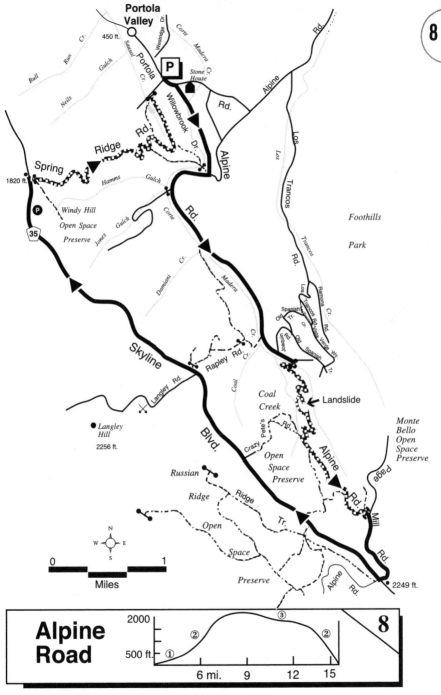

Portola
Valley

450 ft.

P

Stone
House

Westridge Dr.

Corte

Madera Cr.

Rd.

Alpine

Bull

Run

Gulch

Nells

Cr.

Sausal

Portola

Cr.

Willowbrook Dr.

Ridge

Rd.

Alpine

Rd.

Los

Los

Trancos

Foothills

Park

Spring

1820 ft.

P

35

Hamms

Gulch

Gulch

Corte

Windy Hill

Open Space

Preserve

Jones

Gulch

Domiani

Cr.

Madera

Cr.

Cr.

Trancos

Rd.

Trancos

Ramona

Cr.

Los

Trancos

Rd.

Spanish

Tr.

Cr.

Old

Vista Verde

Wy.

Spanish

Rd.

Old

Rd.

Humboldt

Old

Spanish

Tr.

Skyline

Rapley

Rd.

Cr.

Coal

Coal

Creek

← Landslide

Langley Rd.

Langley
Hill

2256 ft.

Crazy

Pete's

Rd.

Open
Space
Preserve

Alpine

Rd.

Monte
Bello
Open
Space
Preserve

Blvd.

Russian

Ridge

Ridge

Open

Space

Preserve

Tr.

Alpine

Rd.

Page

Mill

Rd.

2249 ft.

N
W E
S

0   1

Miles

Alpine
Road

2000

500 ft.

① ② ③ ②

6 mi.   9   12   15

8

8 been graded and improved by MROSD. It's an easy descent now, but use caution while descending on this popular hiking trail.

As you ride down Windy Hill, note how poor soil and constant movement of the subsoil has stifled tree growth. Windy Hill was given its name by the U.S. Geological Survey in the 1960s. It was originally called Spring Hill, for its many springs, but Windy Hill is aptly named for those ocean breezes.

Long Ridge

9

DISTANCE >>> 14 miles

TERRAIN >>> Hilly with one major climb

TRAFFIC >>> Bicyclists, hikers, equestrians

HOW TO GET THERE >>> From Highway 85, take the DeAnza Boulevard exit going south. Becomes Saratoga-Sunnyvale Road. Go about 4 miles to Saratoga. Right at traffic light onto Highway 9 (Big Basin Way) in downtown Saratoga. Drive 6.2 miles up to Skyline Boulevard. Parking available at the Skyline overlook across Highway 9 from the trailhead.

LONG RIDGE, OFF SKYLINE BOULEVARD on the Peninsula, has enough trails to keep riders busy for many rides to come. This ride offers numerous options. You can make it a short, easy ride or a long, hard one going the full distance—or anything in between. For those who like climbing, Charcoal Road's 20-percent grade can't be beat! Here's your chance to practice wheel spin and front-wheel liftoffs. Most of the ride suits mountain bike riders of intermediate ability, with a just a few technical sections.

The ride starts off with 2 miles of single-track on Saratoga Gap Trail, and it won't put you to sleep. The trail parallels Skyline Boulevard, rolling up and down through a dense forest of redwoods and madrone. Rock outcroppings and exposed tree roots will test less experienced riders in a few places.

On the west side of Skyline Boulevard you'll follow the rolling Long Ridge Road. The trail switches back and forth from road to single-track across exposed ridges with spectacular views of the peninsula and the Coast Range.

At 3.5 miles you'll have the option of taking Peters Creek Trail. It's closed in the winter due to marshy conditions along the creek and doesn't open until late spring. The trail goes past a small reservoir and continues gently downhill to Peters Creek.

Stay on Long Ridge Road for a longer ride. Where Long Ridge Road ends, pick up a smooth single-track and roll along before descending

San Francisco and Peninsula << 51

9 MILEAGE LOG

0.0 Start mileage at trailhead off the north side of Highway 9, about 25 yards from the junction with Skyline.

1.7 Keep straight crossing Charcoal Road, continuing on trail.

2.0 Keep straight crossing Skyline Boulevard, continuing at trailhead.

2.2 Right at T junction onto Long Ridge Road.

2.3 Left at Y junction on signed trail.

2.4 Left at Y junction.

2.6 Left onto Long Ridge Road.

3.2 Right at Y junction onto Hickory Oak Trail.

3.4 Left onto Long Ridge Road. 3.5 Peters Creek Trail on right.

4.0 Right onto single-track Long Ridge Trail. Long Ridge Road ends.

4.7 Keep straight at junction. Hard right goes to Peters Creek Trail. 5.0 Cross private dirt road and continue on trail. Begin steep descent to Peters Creek.

5.4 Sharp left at junction. Cross bridge over Peters Creek. Begin gradual climb on single-track trail that parallels Portola Heights Road.

6.0 Right at wooden gate. Continue straight to Skyline Boulevard, riding around iron gate for Portola Heights Road.

6.02 Right onto Skyline Boulevard.

6.4 Left at parking lot to Grizzly Flat Trail. Keep left at Y junction beginning trail. Begin steep descent.

8.3 Left at signed trail junction to Canyon Trail. Straight goes down to Stevens Creek, a dead end. 8.4 Ford Stevens Creek. Begin climb on single-track with several tight switchbacks.

8.8 Right onto Stevens Canyon Trail at T junction.

9.1 Right at Y junction to Saratoga Gap Trail. 9.12 Ford Stevens Creek and begin steep climb on single-track trail. Poison oak grows along trail.

10.2 Right on Table Mountain Road at T junction.

10.7 Right onto Charcoal Road at T junction.

11.5 Right at T junction, continuing on dirt road.

12.3 Left at junction onto Saratoga Gap Trail, returning to start.

14.0 End ride at Highway 9 trailhead.

---

steeply on a wide trail to Peters Creek. Take the single-track Bay Area Ridge Trail back up to Skyline Boulevard.

Return on Skyline a short distance to begin one of the best descents in the Bay Area, Grizzly Flat Trail. It's 2 miles of smooth, rut-free dirt passing through a beautiful grove of towering Douglas fir. Watch for hikers and other bike riders coming uphill.

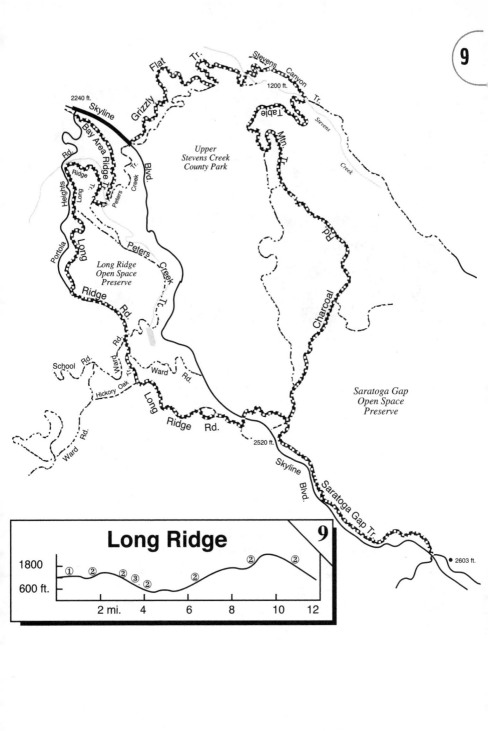

Flat Tr.

Stevens Canyon Tr.

Grizzly

2240 ft.

Skyline

Bay Area Ridge

Rd.

Ridge

Heights

Long Tr.

Creek

Peters

Blvd.

1200 ft.

Table

Mtn. Tr.

Stevens Creek

Upper Stevens Creek County Park

Rd.

Charcoal

Portola

Long

Peters

Long Ridge Open Space Preserve

Creek Tr.

Ridge Rd.

Rd.

Dam Tr.

School Rd.

Hickory Oak Tr.

Ward Rd.

Long

Ward Rd.

Ridge Rd.

Saratoga Gap Open Space Preserve

2520 ft.

Skyline Blvd.

Saratoga Gap Tr.

• 2603 ft.

Long Ridge

9

1800

600 ft.

① ② ② ③ ② ② ②

2 mi. 4 6 8 10 12

From Long Ridge you can see the Coast Range north to San Francisco.

Once down the hill, ford Stevens Creek and climb from the canyon floor; the San Andreas Fault passes through here. Several tight switchbacks lead up to Stevens Canyon Trail, where you'll go right and downhill back to Stevens Creek for another crossing sans bridge.

The ride up is one-way, with the first mile on a narrow single-track through dense growths of Douglas fir and redwoods. Poison oak grows along the trail in the first half-mile, so this ride is best done in the early spring or fall. In the summer you'll be pestered by tiny black flies.

The trail levels out after about a half-mile and becomes a much easier climb. However, the easy riding ends abruptly at Table Mountain Trail. It will take a superhuman effort to ride all the way to Skyline Boulevard. Expect to walk about halfway, or even more. Fortunately, it's a pleasant hike through the forest, and afterwards you'll notice that hills you once thought of as hard climbs pale in comparison to what you've just experienced.

Purisima Creek Road

DISTANCE >>> 21 miles

TERRAIN >>> Hilly

TRAFFIC >>> Bicyclists, hikers, equestrians, light to moderate car traffic

HOW TO GET THERE >>> From Interstate 280, take the Highway 92 exit west. At the summit of Highway 92, turn left onto Skyline Boulevard. It's 5 miles to the Midpeninsula Regional Open Space District parking lot on the right.

PURISIMA CREEK CANYON, IN Purisima Creek Open Space Preserve, was clear-cut in the late 1800s. Fortunately, today we can enjoy the tranquil beauty of the lower canyon, with its 80-year-old redwood groves, fern-draped canyon walls, and burbling Purisima Creek.

The woodsmen made dozens of logging roads for their oxen to drag logs to mills in the Coast Range. Purisima Creek Road is one such logging road. Rufus Hatch and George Borden began logging the canyon in the 1850s; a sawmill in the lower canyon operated until the early 1920s. Logging trucks used the road again in the 1960s and 1970s.

Start riding from the Purisima Creek Midpeninsula Regional Open Space District parking lot on Skyline Boulevard, 2.4 miles north of Kings Mountain Road. Take the steep Harkins Fire Trail to the bottom of Purisima Canyon, ride west to the coast on Higgins Purisima Road, turn south on Highway 1, and finish by riding up Purisima Canyon.

Early in the ride, you'll skirt the upper reaches of Whittemore Gulch on a narrow trail on the way to Harkins Fire Trail. Harkins has views of the ocean and brush-covered ridges, but on a summer day the coast can be fogged in. It can be sweltering on Skyline while damp and cool in the canyon.

Leave the park on Higgins Purisima Road after crossing Purisima Creek on a wooden bridge. San Mateo County paved the road in 1987. Turn right and climb for a half-mile before descending to Highway 1. Vegetable fields line the coast. In a field on the left, look for the white-frame Johnston house, built in 1853 by James Johnston. Johnston made his fortune as a land speculator and saloon keeper in San Francisco. He and his three brothers built the first road from the bay to the coast through Pilarcitos Valley, just north of Highway 92.

Half Moon Bay is only a mile to the north and can be reached by turning right off Highway 1 onto Main Street. There's a bakery, a well-stocked general store, and a bike shop downtown. West of town you'll find the former Ocean Shore Railroad station on Railroad Avenue (see Mileage Log). The railroad, which reached Tunitas Creek, was established in 1905 by land speculators who hoped to develop the coast from San Francisco to Santa Cruz, but it failed to catch on and was shut down in 1920.

From Higgins Purisima Road, ride south on Highway 1 to the junction of Purisima Creek Road. Purisima thrived at this junction at the turn of the century, but all that remains today is a cypress grove. As

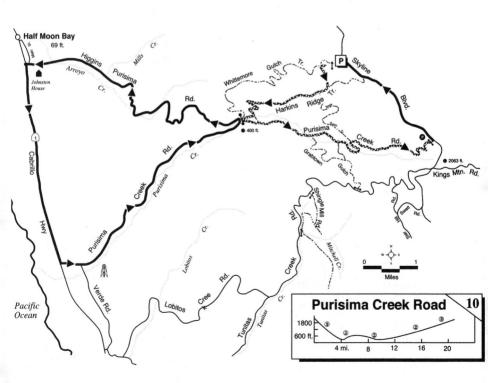

Purisima Creek Road **10**

MILEAGE LOG

0.0 Start mileage at the Midpeninsula Regional Open Space District parking lot on Skyline Boulevard, 2.4 miles north of Kings Mountain Road in San Mateo County. Leave parking lot and go west on trail. Restooms on right just beyond the trailhead entrance.

0.3 Left on narrow trail at four-way junction.

0.9 Right on Harkins Fire Trail at T junction. Begin steep descent. 1.24 Soda Gulch Trail on left.

3.1 Keep right at junction near Purisima Creek.

3.3 Left at T junction onto bridge over Purisima Creek, then immediate right on Purisima Creek Trail after crossing bridge.

3.4 Right on paved Higgins Purisima Road after exiting parking lot.

7.8 Left on Highway 1 at stop sign.

(To reach railroad station: 0.0 Right on Main Street at Highway 1. 0.4 Left on Poplar Street. 1.1 Left on Railroad Avenue (building on right). 1.2 Left on Grove Street. 1.6 Right on Highway 1.)

9.8 Cowell Ranch Beach access on right.

11.0 Left on Verde Road. 11.3 Purisima town site on left.

11.4 Keep straight at junction. Becomes Purisima Creek Road. 12.5 Oil well on right in field.

14.9 Right into parking lot for Purisima Creek trailhead. 14.93 Gate. Begin climb to Skyline. 16.0 Grabtown Gulch Trail on right. Goes to Tunitas Creek Road. 16.1 Cross creek on bridge. 16.4 Cross creek on bridge. 16.8 Cross creek on bridge. 17.1 Cross creek (culvert) and begin steep climb. Next mile is the steepest. 17.3 Soda Gulch Trail on left. 19.07 Gate.

19.1 Left on Skyline Boulevard. 19.5 Richards Road trail on right. 19.8 Snack bar.

21.1 End ride at parking lot.

---

you pass Verde Road, look for an oil derrick to the right on the far hill. The derrick was the first oil well in San Mateo County, yielding forty thousand barrels of oil from 1867 to 1948. Farther up the canyon, horses graze among oil wells in the front yards of ranch houses.

Return to Purisima Canyon at the parking lot, and begin climbing Purisima Creek Trail. The gradient goes from flat to steep and steeper yet. The road steepens even more after crossing Purisima Creek at a left hairpin. The canyon is densely wooded the entire way.

DISTANCE >>> 21 miles

TERRAIN >>> Hilly

TRAFFIC >>> Bicyclists, hikers, equestrians, light car traffic

HOW TO GET THERE >>> From Interstate 280 southbound, take the Foothill Boulevard exit going west for about 2 miles. Take northbound 280 exit at Foothill Boulevard and then go left at the traffic light. Foothill Boulevard becomes Stevens Canyon Road. Go left at the sign into Stevens Canyon Park.

ONE OF THE DEADLIEST PLACES IN the world also makes for great mountain bike riding—the San Andreas Fault. A trail extending the length of Stevens Canyon runs directly over the this fault, which was responsible for the 1906 San Francisco earthquake. The canyon trail has a long history. In the late 1800s, loggers used oxen to haul redwood logs on "skid roads" in the canyon. More recently, farmers used the road to tend orchards on the surrounding ridges.

The ride starts in Stevens Creek County Park, an old ranch site, and former site of Villa Maria winery a few miles west of Cupertino. Santa Clara University used the winery from 1872 to 1944. The first settler in the area, Captain Elisha Stephens, arrived in 1850. Park headquarters, down the hill from the parking lot, has a small museum.

After riding along Stevens Canyon Road past Stevens Creek Reservoir—an earthen dam built in 1936—you'll begin a long climb on Montebello Road, which has an average grade of 7 to 8 percent. The first mile is the steepest, with one short pitch of 15 percent. On the way up, you'll pass the Picchetti and Ridge wineries. The Picchetti property is leased from the Midpeninsula Regional Open Space District (MROSD) by Sunrise Winery in Boulder Creek. MROSD, a public land agency, maintains the ranch and winery, built in the 1870s. The historic site includes a wine cellar and old wine equipment. Wine tastings are held Friday, Saturday, and Sunday, 11 A.M. to 3 P.M.

Ridge Winery, located in an old ranch house overlooking Santa Clara Valley high up on Montebello Ridge, invites wine tasters on Saturdays. Established in the late 1800s, this prestigious winery shut

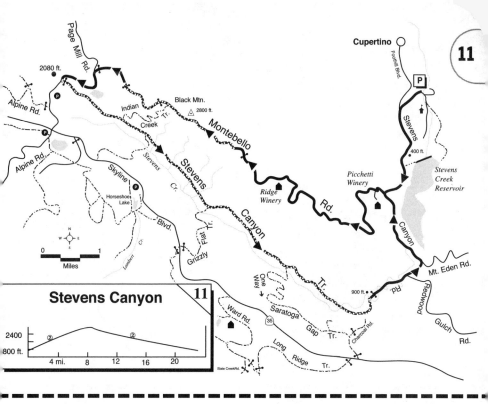

down for a time but was revived in 1962 by two Palo Alto residents. They sold the winery in 1987.

It's another mile from Ridge Winery to a locked gate you can walk your bike around. The pavement ends shortly after the gate. The final climb to the Black Mountain summit goes over a ridge with views of the Coast Range and San Francisco Bay. If you want to cut the ride short, descend Indian Creek Trail to Stevens Canyon Trail. To do so, take the first left on a ranch road as you descend from the top of Black Mountain. You'll find the trailhead sign about 0.3 miles down the road, next to a ranch house. Indian Creek Trail is a wide, steep road.

For the measured ride, continue north, mostly downhill, and turn left when you reach Page Mill Road. Walk your bike through a gap in a black steel gate to reach the road. Stevens Canyon Trail joins Page Mill on the left in a few tenths of a mile. In the next 5 miles you'll descend 1,200 feet on the steep trail. In the dry season, the terrain changes from

11 MILEAGE LOG

0.0 Start mileage at Stevens Creek County Park from first signed parking lot on Stevens Canyon Road. Ride up steep hill for 25 yards and turn left on Stevens Canyon Road. 0.7 Stevens Creek Dam.

1.2 Right on Montebello Road. 1.7 Picchetti Ranch and Sunrise Winery. 2.6 Jimsomare vineyard. 5.6 Ridge Winery on left. 6.4 Locked gate. Continue north on paved road, which soon turns to dirt. 8.0 Black Mountain summit with microwave towers.

8.5 Keep right at junction. Go left at junction for 0.1 miles if you want water from a spigot at the backpack camp. 9.5 Locked gate. Continue straight.

10.0 Left on Page Mill Road at locked gate.

10.5 Left at entrance to signed Stevens Canyon Trail.

11.7 Keep right at Indian Creek Trail junction.

13.6 Keep straight at Grizzly Flat Trail junction.

14.0 Left up trail. Note Saratoga Gap Trail junction on right in circular clearing. 14.4 Ford Stevens Creek. 14.7 Wooden barrier. 14.8 Stevens Canyon Road begins. 15.1 Cross Stevens Creek, pouring over road. 17.2 Redwood Gulch Road intersection and stop sign.

18.8 Left at stop sign. Mt. Eden Road on right.

21.4 End ride at parking lot.

---

meadows of golden wild oats higher up to oaks, buckeye, tan oak, and finally redwoods and Douglas fir deep in the damp, dark canyon.

Telltale signs of sinkholes and distorted earth can be seen 200 yards after taking Stevens Canyon Trail at Page Mill Road. On the left, in a thicket of willows, is a sag pond that's choked with lilies.

Deep in the canyon, you'll come to a circular clearing where there's a one-way trail sign for Saratoga Gap on the right. Take the narrow trail on the left, going uphill. Watch out for poison oak. After a short, steep descent, you'll ford Stevens Creek and cross a landslide. Cross Stevens Creek once again (it spills over the paved road), and you're back on pavement. It's mostly downhill to Stevens Creek Reservoir. Stevens Canyon can be enjoyed year-round, but it's especially nice on hot days or in fall when the leaves are turning. Helmets are required on this ride.

Almaden Quicksilver County Park

12

DISTANCE >>> 10 miles

TERRAIN >>> One big climb and descent, then level

TRAFFIC >>> Bicyclists, hikers, equestrians

HOW TO GET THERE >>> From the 85 freeway in San Jose, take the Almaden Expressway exit south. Stay in the ramp's middle lane, make the first left, then the next right onto Almaden Expressway. Go about 4 miles to Almaden Road and turn right at the traffic light. Continue on Almaden Road for about 3 miles to New Almaden. The Hacienda entrance is at the west end of town on the right. There's plenty of parking.

THANKS TO OPEN-MINDED OFFICIALS in Santa Clara County, bicycles were allowed on a trial basis in 1999 at Almaden Quicksilver County Park, and in 2001 the county officially sanctioned bicycling in the park. This loop ride touches all parts of the 3,977-acre park and covers just about every foot of trail open for bicycling. The climbs and descents are nontechnical and only moderately steep.

After a steady 3-mile climb you're rewarded with a beautiful winding descent and views of Guadalupe Reservoir, the Coast Range, and Santa Clara Valley. The ride back on Randol Trail rolls along and then levels out before the final 1-mile descent to the park's Hacienda entrance.

Blue oaks dominate the landscape, offering substantial shade on the climb to Bull Run summit. In the spring, wildflowers carpet the rocky ground, including lupine and Indian paintbrush. At the summit there's a picnic table where you can sit and take in the view to the southwest of Mt. Umunhum and its concrete blockhouse, a former Air Force radar station.

After a fun descent to Mine Hill Trail, from which you can see Guadalupe Reservoir below to the west, the ride eases up. Randol Trail narrows somewhat as it snakes away along the park's east ridge. Mine tailings can be seen at the Day Tunnel on the left side of the road, but the mine is closed, as are all of the park's mine shafts.

It's almost impossible to tell that the land you're riding through supported a thriving mining community until the 1940s. Almost every trace of the New Almaden Mines has been removed, and vegetation covers once barren hillsides. Look for a tall brick chimney at the Hacienda entrance, all that remains of a massive reduction factory.

At the peak of the mining era, more than eighteen hundred miners and their families lived in neighborhoods of different ethnicities— Spanish, Cornish, Chinese, English. They mined cinnabar, a red ore smelted in huge furnaces to yield mercury. The silvery liquid metal played a vital role in the California gold rush, as it was needed for smelting gold ore.

An impressive collection of mining equipment and photos of the early days can be viewed at the New Almaden Museum on Almaden Road, located in the Casa Grande, a three-story mansion built in 1854. It's just under a half-mile east of the Hacienda entrance. Hours are Friday, noon to 4 P.M., Saturday and Sunday 10 A.M. to 4 P.M.; phone (408) 323-1107.

Hacienda is the only entrance open to bicycles and offers the only drinking water. Helmets are required.

Mine Hill Road looking north brings the South Bay and Guadalupe Reservoir into view.

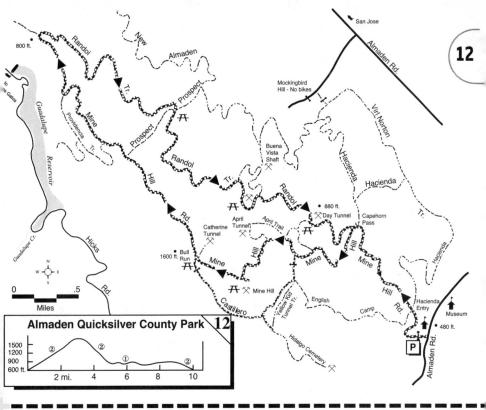

MILEAGE LOG

0.0 Start mileage at the iron gate to Mine Hill Trail. Follow signs to Bull Run summit. It's a steady climb on a dirt road. 0.4 English Camp Trail and Hacienda Trail junctions.

1.1 Keep left staying on Mine Hill Trail at junction with Randol Trail and Capehorn Pass.

1.7 Right at Y junction. Unsigned. Castillero Trail on left.

1.8 Keep left at Y junction. April Trail on right.

1.9 Keep left at Y junction. April Trail on right again. 2.3 San Cristobal Mine Trail on left.

2.6 Right on Mine Hill Trail at summit, beginning descent. Castillero Trail comes in from left. 3.4 Prospect Trail on right. 3.7 Providencia Trail on left. 4.3 Providencia Trail on left again.

4.7 Right on Randol Trail. 6.2 Prospect Trail on right. 7.4 Santa Isabel Trail junction. Stay on Randol. 7.9 Buena Vista Trail on left. 8.5 Day Tunnel on right.

9.0 Right onto Mine Hill Trail at Capehorn Pass junction. Begin descent.

10.1 End ride back at parking lot.

13 Gazos Creek Road

DISTANCE >>> 28 miles

TERRAIN >>> Hilly

TRAFFIC >>> Bicyclists, hikers, equestrians

HOW TO GET THERE >>> From Interstate 280, take Highway 85 south. On Highway 85 take the Saratoga Avenue exit, west. Saratoga Avenue becomes Highway 9, Big Basin Way. Continue west to Skyline Boulevard. Keep straight, and in another 6 miles take the Highway 236 exit and follow the winding, narrow road to Big Basin Redwoods State Park (see Big Basin Redwood's State Park road ride).

BIG BASIN REDWOODS STATE PARK HAS some of the most dramatic and primitive off-road riding anywhere in the Bay Area. The word has gotten out among mountain bike riders, and now this venue draws cyclists of all abilities. On this tour you'll see burbling creeks and ancient redwoods, and experience whoop-de-doos; you'll even cross an airstrip on a lonely mountain ridge.

Road conditions change with the season. Gazos Creek Road can become a sand pit in the summer, especially after grading. A tour of the road after the winter floods of 1982–83 was an arduous hike over fallen redwoods and boulders. Nearly a mile of road was wiped off the map when Gazos Creek turned from a peaceful stream to a raging torrent.

The ride starts at park headquarters and immediately hits dirt on Gazos Creek Road, where you'll have a gentle climb followed by a brisk descent among redwoods and Douglas fir. At the bottom of the first descent, notice downed trees on the hillside to the right. The trees toppled as the earth crept down the hill. Redwoods grow to more than 200 feet, but their shallow roots make them susceptible to land movements and strong winds.

At 6 miles, the Sandy Point Guard Station junction (the station burned down in the 1960s) is a popular turnaround point. After a steep descent on Gazos Creek Road, the only way back is to continue the ride or return on Gazos Creek Road. The road becomes rutted and bumpy, and it can be muddy in the spring. It's hard to believe, but until the mid-1960s, the road was open to car traffic.

Gazos Creek Road crosses through a beautiful redwood grove.

If you continue, after the wild, steep descent you'll reach a gate, followed by pavement. San Mateo County paved the section between here and Cloverdale Road in the summer of 1992. The remaining miles to Cloverdale Road are nothing less than heavenly as you follow the

MILEAGE LOG

0.0 Start mileage at the junction of Gazos Creek Road and North Escape Road about a quarter-mile north of Big Basin Redwoods State Park headquarters on Highway 236. (The park's food store rents mountain bikes.) Gazos Creek Road immediately crosses a bridge over Opal Creek. 0.1 Locked gate. 0.9 Middle Ridge Road on right; you'll return on this road. 3.0 Open gate.

6.1 Right at Sandy Point Guard Station. Whitehouse Canyon Road to left. 6.2 Johansen Fire Road. Second gate on right after passing open area. 8.1 Gate at bottom of hill. 8.3 Bridge over Gazos Creek. 9.7 Log dam artifact in Gazos Creek.

11.5 Right on Cloverdale Road. Unsigned. 12.7 Butano State Park entrance. Water available inside park, 0.3 miles from entrance.

13.6 Right onto Butano Fire Trail at paved ramp that goes uphill 15 yards to a locked aluminum gate. Lift bike over gate. Unsigned.

16.2 Keep right at junction. 16.8 Gate, usually open. 18.7 Cross airstrip. 19.3 Butano Trail Camp on right. 19.7 Olmo Fire Road on right. 19.8 Open gate.

22.7 Right at junction onto China Grade. Locked cable across road.

23.2 Right on Johansen Road.

24.1 Left on Middle Ridge Fire Road. 24.3 Locked gate. 26.1 Dooly Trail.

26.6 Left on Gazos Creek Road.

27.5 End ride at park headquarters.

gently flowing creek under a canopy of sycamore, ash, maple, and Pacific dogwood.

In the late 1890s, Gazos Creek had a completely different complexion. It was dammed and used as a log pen for a sawmill near the road. Remnants of the redwood dam on the creek bank are still visible from the road.

Turn right onto Cloverdale Road, which was paved from the ocean to Butano State Park in 1987. Your next turn is not marked, so look carefully for Butano Fire Road where it joins Cloverdale. There's a short, steep paved driveway leading to an aluminum gate, about 1 mile north of the Butano park entrance. The dirt road beyond the gate climbs an exposed ridge before entering a wooded canyon with

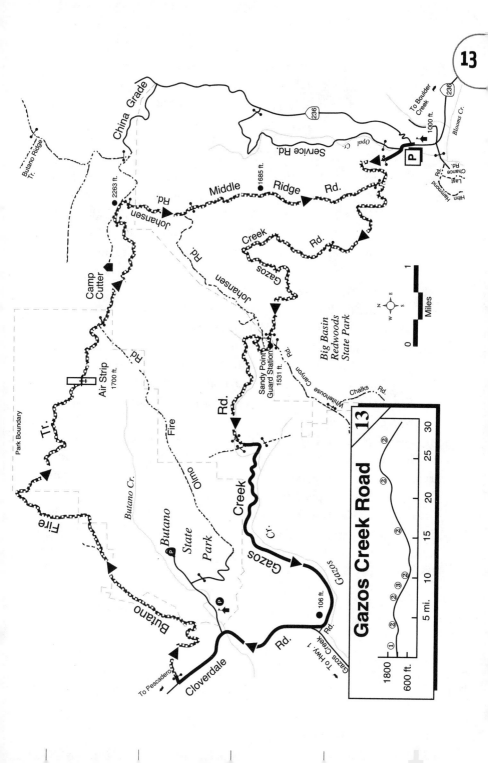

Butano Fire Trail climbs more than 2,000 feet from the ocean.

impressive stands of Douglas fir. The lower part of the canyon features dense foliage of brambles and poison oak.

With one exception—noted in the Mileage Log—Butano Fire Road has no road junctions. Along the way, the scenery changes from tree-covered slopes to exposed ridges of granulated shale. Redwoods give way to knobcone pines on the dry, rocky ridges. The road becomes a smooth bed of loose white shale leading up to an airstrip. After crossing the airstrip you'll have a brief descent into a dark forest, followed by more, and steeper, climbing.

China Grade, altitude 2,265 feet, marks the summit. Turn right at the wire cable crossing the road. (There's a Boy Scout camp to the left.) Take China Grade, which was paved at one time, to Johansen Road, the next junction. Descend about a mile and turn left on Middle Ridge Road. It's a roller-coaster ride to Gazos Creek over sandstone and sand pits that rival anything at Spy Glass. At Gazos Creek Road, turn left and return to park headquarters. Don't miss the park headquarters interpretive center across Highway 236 from the park's concession stand.

Thanks to Andrew Hill, a San Jose artist and photographer, this area became a park in 1902. In 1900, Hill founded the Sempervirens Club to help create a park, raising money and lobbying to preserve old-growth redwoods. The club was revived as the Sempervirens Fund in 1968, when developers threatened to build on private land inside the park. The fund, based in Los Altos, has raised money to help expand the park to 19,000 acres.

Henry W. Coe State Park

DISTANCE >>> 16 miles

TERRAIN >>> Extremely hilly

TRAFFIC >>> Bicyclists, hikers, equestrians

HOW TO GET THERE >>> From Highway 101, take the Dunne Avenue exit, east. It's about 13 miles to the park headquarters, which has limited parking. Parking costs $2.

HENRY W. COE STATE PARK WOULD be a suitable location for an episode of *Survivor*. The park's remote trails and steep roads test the best riders' abilities. Don't ride here unless you know how to handle a bike, are a strong rider, and are safety conscious. In the event of an accident, it could be many hours before a rescue in this enormous park. In fact, a mountain bike rider got lost in the late 1990s; he managed to find his way to a paved road after two days.

Our state's second largest park, Henry Coe encompasses nearly 100 square miles (80,000 acres). More than 200 miles of ranch roads and trails touch every section of the park, although mountain bikes are prohibited in the Orestimba Wilderness Area. Nearly every road is either straight up or straight down. In the spring, you can take a break during the ride and enjoy the park's spectacular wildflower display. In the fall you'll have autumn colors and cool, crisp air. Weather can be severe—brutally hot and freezing cold. Water is available at park headquarters only.

This route makes a figure-eight loop, with two sections of single-track. The rest of the ride takes dirt roads. Always expect to encounter other trail users around the next turn. Note that Middle Ridge Trail is closed to mountain bikes for 48 hours after significant rains. As a precaution, check in with the ranger before riding and check back in when you leave. If you do run into trouble, the ranger will know you're out there.

Start at a yellow gate across the paved road from park headquarters. Take Pacheco Route for four-tenths of a mile and turn left,

14

MILEAGE LOG

0.0 Start mileage at Pacheco Route, the yellow gate opposite the park headquarters.

0.4 Left at Northern Heights Route to monument, uphill. 0.9 Monument on right. 1.0 Begin descent to Frog Lake. (Take trail at mile 1.6 to visit lake; otherwise stay left on road.) 1.9 Begin climb.

2.8 Right on Middle Ridge Trail. View point straight ahead. 3.1 Frog Lake junction on right. 4.3 Fish Trail junction on right. 5.0 Begin steep descent. 6.4 Middle Fork Coyote Creek.

6.6 Left on Pacheco Route. 7.9 Trailhead on left. You'll return here. 8.1 Los Cruzeros camp junction on right.

9.1 Keep left at junction. Begin climb on Northern Heights Route.

9.9 Left at clearing. Go 20 feet and turn left again on Jackass Trail. Right at trail marker, uphill. 10.1 Begin descent.

11.3 Right back onto Pacheco Route. 12.7 Begin climb.

14.4 Keep right. Manzanita Point junction on left.

16.0 End ride at park headquarters.

---

uphill. Northern Heights Route rises steeply across an exposed ridge. Look for a granite monument dedicated to Henry Coe at the summit under some pine trees.

Descend for about a mile to Frog Lake. The road circles the small lake, which is out of sight below you. There's a gradual climb to the Deerhorn Viewpoint and Middle Ridge Trail. Middle Ridge begins just before the overlook on the right, at the "Frog Lake" marker.

The overlook reveals a breathtaking view of Blue Ridge and the perilously steep Short Cut Road. After taking in the view, turn around and pick up Middle Ridge Trail. The trail rolls along for the next 2 miles before dropping steeply to the Middle Fork of Coyote Creek. Keep left at the two junctions. The rocky creek is fun to ford when there's water during wet spring months. Ride a short distance to Pacheco Route and turn left. Continue east up Jackass Peak from Poverty Flat backpack camp; there's a steep climb of less than a mile. On the other side of the ridge, at Miller Field, you'll have a couple of steep hills. Keep left at the three major junctions. After the third junction, you'll climb Northern Heights Route for about a mile.

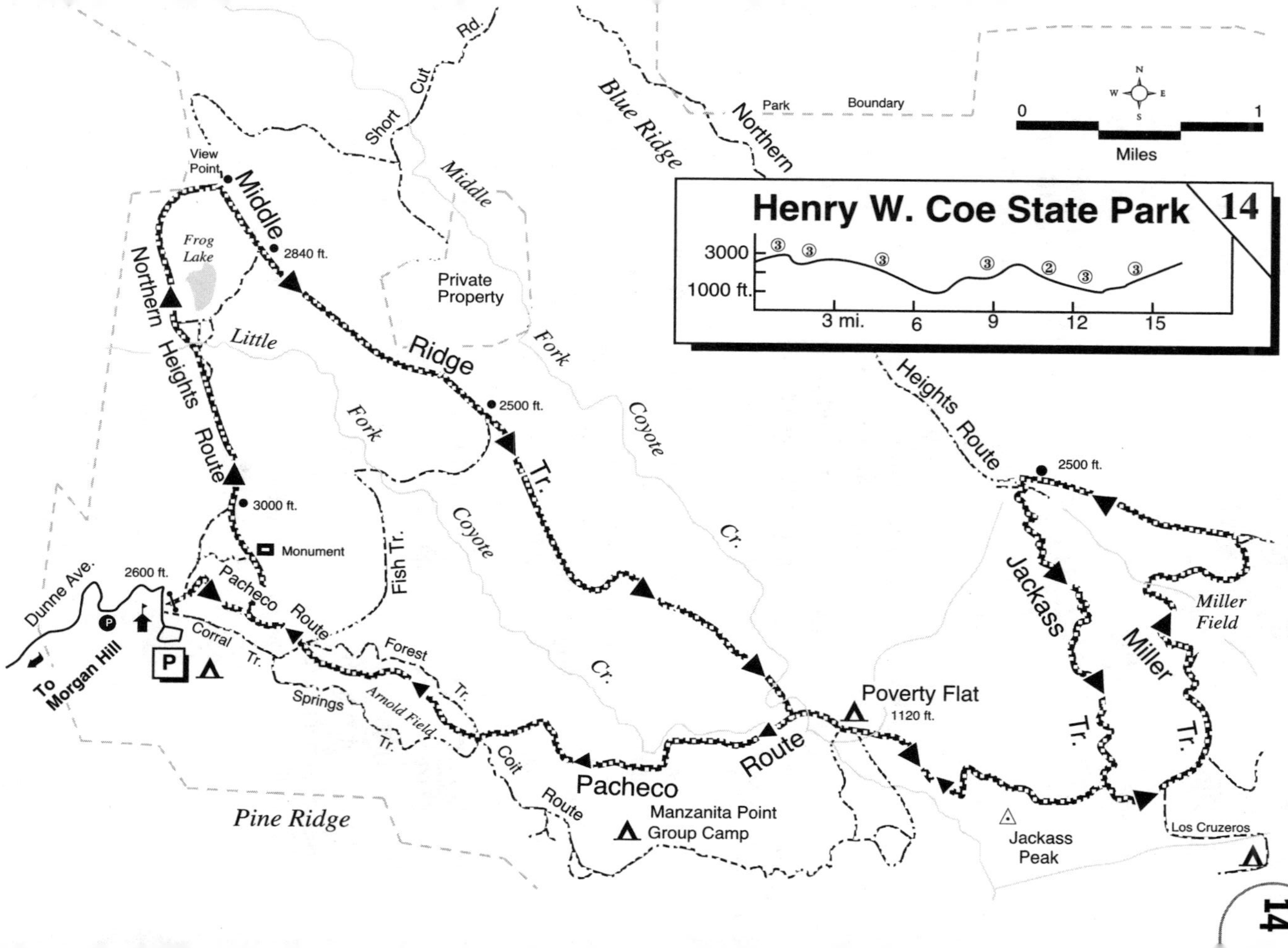

Henry W. Coe State Park 14

N
W — E
S

Miles

0   1

3000 ft.
1000 ft.

3 mi.   3   6   9   12   15

Northern Park Boundary

Blue Ridge

Miller Field

Miller Tr.

Los Cruzeros

Jackass Tr.

Jackass Peak

2500 ft.

Heights Route

Poverty Flat
1120 ft.

Coyote Cr.

Pacheco Route

Manzanita Point
Group Camp

Coyote Fork

Middle Fork

Private Property

2500 ft.

Ridge Tr.

Short Cut Rd.

Coyote Cr.

Colt Route

Forest Tr.

Arnold Field Tr.

Fish Tr.

Springs Tr.

Pacheco Route

View Point

2840 ft.

Middle

Little Fork

Frog Lake

Monument

3000 ft.

Northern Heights Route

Corral Tr.

P

2600 ft.

To Morgan Hill

Dunne Ave.

Pine Ridge

14

Henry W. Coe State Park's steep terrain will cause even the strongest rider to dismount and walk once in a while.

To find the single-track trail, watch the left side of the road and check your cyclometer (see Mileage Log). After riding through oak trees on a steep section, you'll come to a flat spot where there's a small clearing on the left. Go west about 20 feet off the road and pick up Jackass Trail running north-south. Go left on the trail, and begin climbing through some oak trees. In about 50 yards you'll come to a trail post. Turn right onto the trail and continue climbing. Soon you'll reach a clearing with a splendid view of the park to the south and west. The trail winds down the hill through mesquite and open meadows, bringing you back to Miller Field and the ranch road.

Return to headquarters by Pacheco Route. The climb from Poverty Flat has two steep sections early on, then the road climbs less steeply to Arnold Field.

The park is named for Henry W. Coe, whose sons and daughters carried on the tradition of raising cattle at nearby Pine Ridge Ranch. Sada Coe, Henry's daughter, donated the ranch to Santa Clara County in 1953. Over the years, several more ranches were added to the park. Cattle ranching continues at several private inholdings. Don't be surprised to see the occasional rancher's truck.

Overnight campgrounds near park headquarters are available, or you can ride into the park to camp at designated sites. Camping reservations are first come, first served.

Poison oak thrives on the park's many steep slopes and canyons. Know what it looks like and avoid it.

Joseph D. Grant County Park

DISTANCE >>> 8 miles

TERRAIN >>> Extremely hilly

TRAFFIC >>> Bicyclists, hikers, equestrians

HOW TO GET THERE >>> From Interstate 680, take the Alum Rock Avenue exit east. Drive about 2 miles before turning right onto Mt. Hamilton Road. It's about 7.5 miles to the park.

JOSEPH D. GRANT COUNTY PARK'S hilly trails will entertain even the most experienced mountain bike rider. In fact, this ride is recommended only for veteran bikers who aren't afraid of riding down hills suitable for advanced ski runs, who aren't deterred by having to walk up steep hills, and who aren't easily bullied by ornery cattle. A mountain bike race held here in the spring makes good use of the terrain.

The ride starts innocently enough as Hotel Trail takes you through Halls Valley on a flat ranch road. Watch out for cow pies. The valley puts on an impressive wildflower display in the spring. But at the Circle Corral, it's time to circle the wagons. The road climbs briskly at about a 15-percent grade and hardly lets up until Eagle Lake. The small, solitary lake offers a welcome respite from the climb.

What goes up must come down. Digger Pine Trail drops steeply to a stream, where you'll pick your way through rocky sections. The road goes straight up and straight down several more times before leveling at a meadow and Bonhoff Trail. Bonhoff is the cliff on your left.

After walking up Bonhoff, you're greeted by a section of fairly level riding between short, steep climbs. At Mt. Hamilton Road you can see where you've been, far below. After some more climbing, you'll turn left onto Yerba Buena Trail and pick your way down to a parking lot at McCreery Lake. The trail is hard to follow in places, because it becomes a cattle trail next to Mt. Hamilton Road. There's one particularly steep, loose spot to watch for as you approach Mt. Hamilton Road and the fence.

The ride may be only 8 miles, but it feels like 50. Helmets are required in all Santa Clara County parks.

MILEAGE LOG

0.0 Start ride at the entrance to Hotel Trail at green gate, located about 50 yards from the white house that serves as Joseph D. Grant County Park headquarters.

0.7 Keep right on Lower Hotel Trail. 1.5 Gate.

1.7 Circle Corral. Ride through corral to green gate. Take road to right on other side of gate. 1.8 Begin steep climb after crossing creek. 2.8 Small pond and brief respite from climb. Cañada De Pala Trail crossing.

3.5 Eagle Lake. Keep left of lake and begin steep descent on Digger Pine Trail.

4.5 Left on Bonhoff Trail. Begin steep climb. Right goes to Smith Creek and fire station.

5.4 Cross Mt. Hamilton Road at green gate and proceed through gate across road. Begin Cañada De Pala Trail.

5.9 Left on Yerba Buena Trail.

8.2 End ride at parking lot for McCreery Lake next to Mt. Hamilton Road.

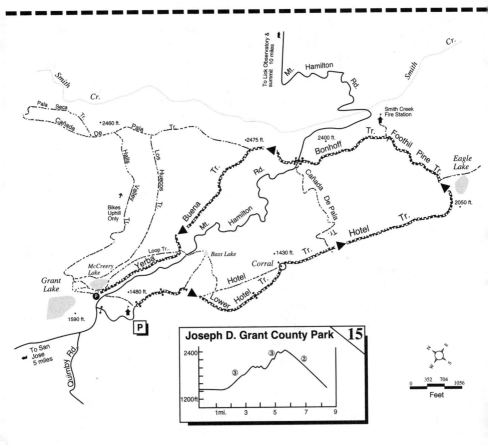

74 >> **Mountain Bike Rides**

Old Haul Road

DISTANCE >>> 18 miles

TERRAIN >>> Gentle grades on the Haul Road; otherwise hilly

TRAFFIC >>> Bicyclists, hikers, equestrians, light car traffic

HOW TO GET THERE >>> From Interstate 280, take the Highway 84 exit west and go through Woodside. Continue over the Coast Range, passing through Loma Mar. Just outside Loma Mar, turn left onto Pescadero Road. Keep right at the sharp turn heading up Haskins Hill, at the Alpine Road intersection. Continue on Pescadero Road over the hill and down to Wurr Road. Turn left at Wurr Road and go three-tenths of a mile, where there's parking at the trailhead.

DEEP IN THE REDWOODS OF SAN Mateo County, there's a railroad right-of-way where a logging train once hauled its heavy load to a sawmill near Highway 9 at Waterman Gap. Today the wail of the train whistle has been replaced by the sound of mountain bike tires riding over gravel. A 42-ton oil-burning Shay locomotive ran between the Santa Cruz Lumber Company sawmill and near Loma Mar from 1921 to 1951, to be replaced by logging trucks until the company sold half its forested lands to public agencies in 1970.

The sale added to the newly formed Pescadero Creek County Park. The county park's eastern boundary joins with Portola State, founded in 1945. The parks have many miles of hiking trails.

In the spring, yellow-flowered Western broom creates an enchanting corridor on the Old Haul Road. There's a scenic view around every bend. Numerous brooks trickle down Butano Ridge and feed into the densely wooded Pescadero Creek. During the winter of 1982–83, these peaceful streams raged out of control, uprooting redwoods and destroying the road. In 1984, work crews from the sheriff's honor farm, located in the park, pitched in to repair the road and clear brush. Today the road is hardpacked, with numerous graveled sections, good for year-round riding. Trail signs mark every junction.

Start your ride next to Memorial Park, which has picnic grounds, camping facilities, restrooms, drinking fountains, and a swimming area.

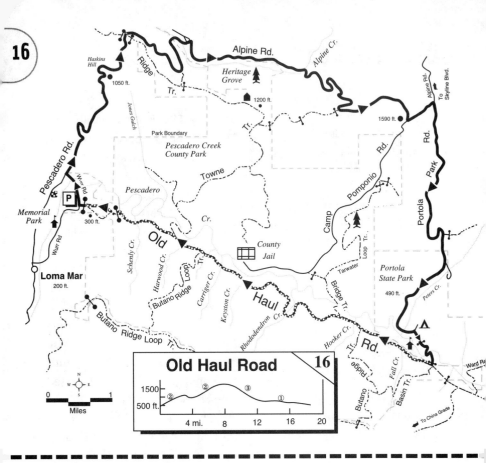

Old Haul Road 16

You'll take Pescadero and Alpine roads, returning through Portola State Park and the Old Haul Road. For a much easier ride, take the Old Haul Road out and back.

Pescadero Road has a 2-mile climb over Haskins Hill, followed by a 1-mile descent to Alpine Road. You'll have 4 miles of uphill before you begin a fast descent to Portola State Park. Inside the park, ride past the campgrounds and pick up the service road. Cross Pescadero Creek on a wooden bridge, and walk your bike a short distance on a narrow trail. Christian Iverson, a Scandinavian immigrant who worked as a Pony Express rider and armed guard, built a log cabin near the Old Haul Road in the 1860s, but it collapsed in the 1989 Loma Prieta earthquake.

MILEAGE LOG

0.0 Start mileage at Old Haul Road Trailhead on Wurr Road, next to Memorial County Park. The trailhead is 0.3 miles south of Pescadero Road and about a half-mile east of the Memorial Park entrance. Ride toward Pescadero Road.

0.3 Right on Pescadero Road at stop sign. 3.0 Haskins Hill summit. 3.8 Entrance to Sam McDonald County Park.

4.3 Right on Alpine Road. 5.6 Heritage Grove old-growth redwoods on right. 6.0 Begin Alpine Road ascent.

8.0 Keep left at Pomponio Road junction and honor camp entrance.

8.4 Right on Portola Park Road at stop sign. Begin descent. 10.6 Portola State Park boundary. 11.8 Park headquarters and interpretive center. Restrooms and water. 12.0 Ride around gate on "Service Area" road.

12.6 Right on narrow trail immediately after crossing bridge over Pescadero Creek. Walk bike. 12.7 Iverson Cabin site. Ride up steep road.

12.8 Right on Old Haul Road at gate.

13.9 Keep left at Bridge Trail junction.

16.7 Left at junction. Crucial intersection. Towne Trail goes straight. No bikes allowed.

17.6 Keep straight and ride around gate.

17.7 Keep right at junction.

18.1 End ride at Wurr Road and locked gate.

The park service has no plans to restore it. Continue on the paved road, which crosses Pescadero Creek and goes up to the Old Haul Road. Turn right at the gate.

Take Bridge Trail if you want to see Pescadero Creek. A Bailey-type bridge spans the creek.

After the ride, there's food and drink waiting at the Loma Mar Store, a mile and a half west of the trailhead on Pescadero Road. You can take Wurr Road or Pescadero Road to get there. The country store has a fireplace, pool table, and TV. You'll enjoy relaxing on the front patio and watching the world go by. For more information, call Pescadero Creek County Park, San Mateo County, (650) 363-4020.

17 Soquel Demonstration Forest

LEGAL SINGLE-TRACK RIDING MAY be almost an oxymoron in the Bay Area, but in the Santa Cruz Mountains there's a 5-mile section of single-track you can ride without worrying about a $270 fine. We have the California Department of Forestry to thank for encouraging mountain biking in the Soquel Demonstration Forest, located on a ridge overlooking Soquel Canyon in Santa Cruz County. Logging interests also deserve recognition, because the logging roads used for harvesting timber are also routes for bicyclists.

The Demonstration Forest shows how trees can be cut responsibly—no clear-cutting here. As you might expect, not everyone agrees, so the park's general plan is an ongoing source of angst for local residents who fear the entire forest will be cut down. The forest was dedicated in 1990, the first to be added to the state forest system since 1949.

It's a 10-mile drive on narrow roads to reach the Demonstration Forest. Highland Way is often blocked by landslides, so you may need to start riding from another location on Highland Way than the one indicated here, or even at Summit School (see Aptos Road ride). In 1998, a massive landslide closed Highland Way, but the more adventurous riders weren't deterred from crossing the slide on foot.

The ride starts with a gradual climb along Soquel Creek at the upper reaches of Soquel Canyon. In the spring it's not unusual to see swarms of ladybugs here. Fog often cloaks the ridge in the summer, and riding through the dark, drippy woods creates an eerie feeling.

The dirt begins on Buzzard Lagoon Road, a well-traveled route for a handful of local residents. You'll have a gradual climb, riding over sections of smooth sandstone, all the way to the start of the single-track. Be sure to turn off Buzzard Lagoon Road after about a mile, staying on the fire road and continuing uphill.

West Ridge Trail slices through the Soquel Demonstration Forest.

About a mile after the Aptos Fire Road gate, look for a wooden kiosk showing a map of the Demonstration Forest. You can also choose to continue on Aptos Creek Fire Road into the Forest of Nisene Marks State Park and ride all the way to Aptos. You'll return the way you came or loop back on San Jose–Soquel Road to Highland Way (see Aptos road ride).

The trails in Demonstration Forest have some steep sections and occasional exposed roots. The steeper sections offer experienced riders a chance to show their skill; the less experienced will choose to walk. Watch out for the occasional poison oak bush, and use caution on the trails. Rescue would be many hours away. Unfortunately, the Demonstration Forest draws more than its share of yahoos, mountain bikers boasting on Web sites about reaching speeds of 35 mph on the trails. On the bright side, other mountain bikers have adopted the forest and maintain the trails.

This ride covers the length of West Ridge Trail, with gradual climbs and descents, except for the last half-mile before Saw Pit Trail. There will be one seriously steep descent on a badly rutted trail, followed by

MILEAGE LOG

0.0 Start mileage at main entrance to the Soquel Demonstration Forest. Look for cars parked on the side of the road and a small bridge crossing Soquel Creek. There is no water on this ride. Ride west on Highland Way, following Soquel Creek. 1.6 Cross Soquel Creek. 1.7 Cross Soquel Creek, continuing somewhat steeper climb.

2.1 Right on Buzzard Lagoon Road, a dirt road, at four-way intersection. Ormsby Trail road is on the left. 2.7 Open gate.

3.1 Keep right at a sharp turn and continue gradual climb where Buzzard Lagoon Road continues straight down a steep grade. This junction isn't marked. Don't miss it! 4.4 Locked gate beginning Aptos Fire Road. 4.6 Begin half-mile descent.

5.4 Right onto West Ridge Trail in Demonstration Forest. Watch for wooden kiosk on right. Begin single-track.

6.0 Left at signed junction with Corral Trail.

6.9 Keep left at helicopter landing site. Trail picks up again in about 100 yards. Sign says "Tractor Trail .9 miles."

7.8 Keep left on West Ridge Trail at junction with Tractor Trail. 8.4 Steep, rutted downhill. Walking allowed. 8.6 Steep climb. Walking required.

8.7 Right on Saw Pit Trail, beginning easier climbing followed by descent. West Ridge Trail ends.

9.9 Left on Hihn's Mill Road at T junction. Begin climb back to Highland Way. 10.5 Tractor Trail on right. 11.9 Sulphur Spring Trail on right. 13.8 Open gate. 14.3 Closed gate.

14.5 End ride at Highland Way.

a short climb that's nearly impossible to pedal up. You have three opportunities for shorter rides, starting with Corral Trail (mostly dirt road), followed by Sulphur Springs Trail (a dirt road) and Tractor Trail (mostly single-track). The single-track ends on Hihn's Mill Road, a well-traveled logging road named for turn-of-the-century timber baron Frederick Hihn. It's all uphill through the redwoods to Highland Way.

Soquel Demonstration Forest
17
2600
2100
1600
1100 ft.
3 mi.
6
9
12
15
West Ridge Tr.
Saw Pit Tr.
①
②
③
③
②
Hwy. 17
10 miles
Soquel
Cr.
Highland
Way
1150 ft.
Not a through road
Sulphur
Springs
Tr.
Pit
Saw
2040 ft.
West
Ridge
Tr.
Tractor
Sulphur
Springs
Tr.
Corral
Tr.
Hihn's
Mill
Rd.
P
1600 ft.
Highland
Way
2531 ft.
Santa Rosalia Mtn.
2629 ft.
Creek
Fire
Rd.
Aptos
Cr.
Hinckley
Aptos
12 miles from West Ridge Trail
Lagoon
Rd.
1900 ft.
Buzzard
Ormsby Tr.
Corralitos
9 miles
N
W
E
S
0
.5
Miles

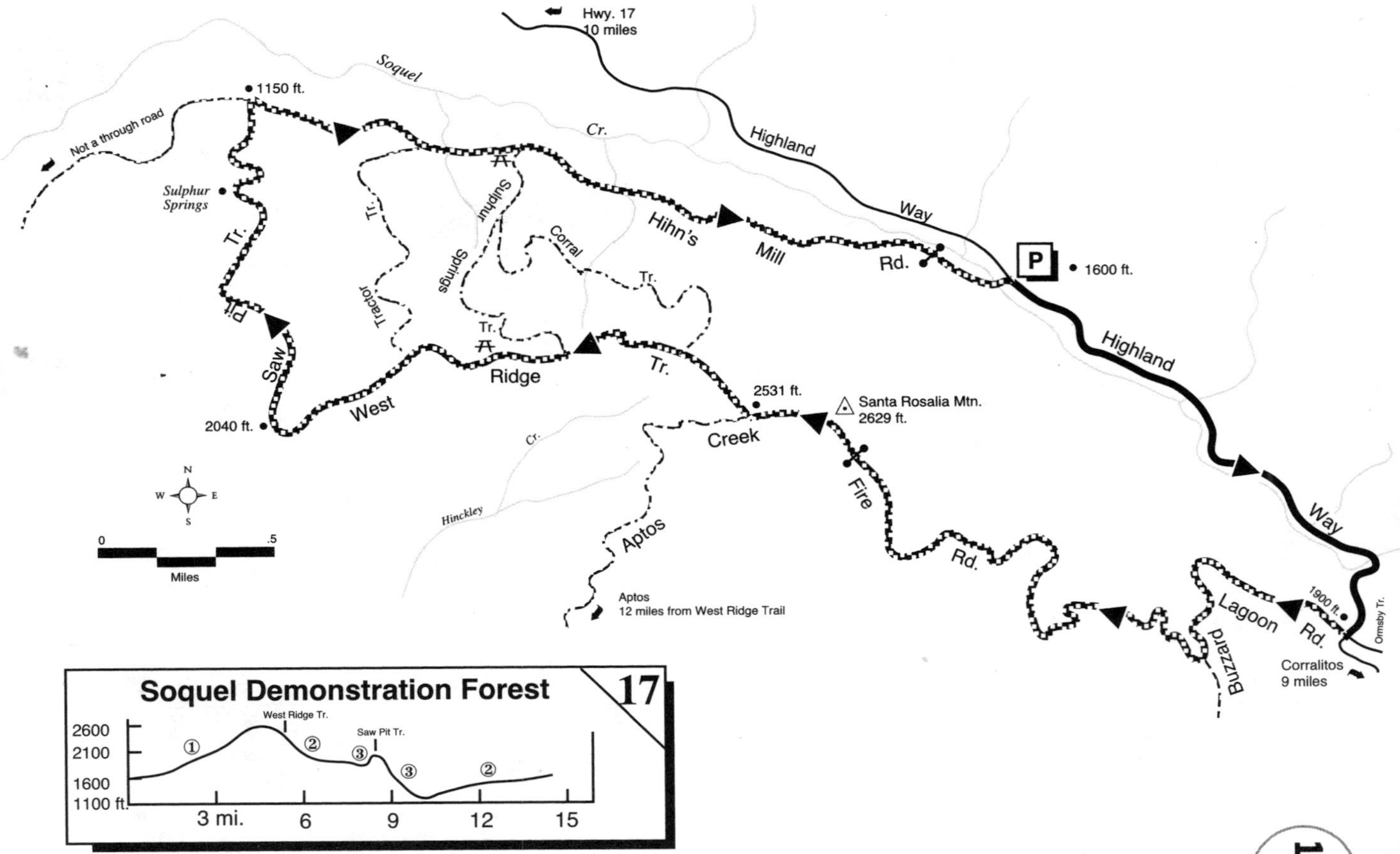

Chileno Valley

DISTANCE >>> 47 miles

TERRAIN >>> Some rolling hills

TRAFFIC >>> Light car traffic, milk trucks

HOW TO GET THERE >>> From Highway 101, take the East Washington Street exit and go west. After about a mile and a half you'll cross the Petaluma River just before reaching Petaluma Boulevard, the community's main street. Take a left at the light and then an immediate right at a light onto Western Avenue. Stay on Western Avenue for about 2 miles to its intersection with Chileno Valley Road, where you'll take a left at the Y intersection. In less than a half-mile you'll turn left into Helen Putnam Park, at the crest of a hill. Parking costs $3.

IF I WERE A BICYCLIST LIVING IN Petaluma, I would count my blessings daily and thank the dairy industry for preserving open space as dairy-cattle countryside. On this ride you'll see rolling, oak-covered hills in Marin and Sonoma counties west of Petaluma, where roads ideal for bicycling wind through lands used primarily for grazing dairy cattle. Petaluma is worth a visit, too. The city has many Victorian-style buildings and other interesting architecture. This unique mix of older buildings drew movie director Francis Ford Coppola to Petaluma to film *Tucker: The Man and His Dream* and *Peggy Sue Got Married.*

On an April day, the roads through green valleys and oak-covered hills are lined with orange and yellow California poppies. Hawks soar overhead, and gobbling wild turkeys can be heard and sometimes seen. The ride includes a hilltop belvedere with expansive views of the narrow Tomales Bay, Point Reyes, and one of the most remote and enchanting roads in the Bay Area, Marshall-Petaluma.

Chileno Valley Road, which you'll cover in its entirety on this ride, enjoys name recognition among local riders for its wide valley and gently rolling hills, but Marshall-Petaluma has its own appeal. It winds through Verde Canyon next to gently flowing creeks hidden by willows and the yellow-flowered Scotch broom. Riding these two roads lets you enjoy in quiet solitude some of the best scenery in Northern California.

All kinds of bikers use Chileno Valley Road.

The ride starts just outside Petaluma at Helen Putnam Regional Park. Take the park's steep, paved multi-use path heading back toward town. Next to the path there's a small pond where red-winged blackbirds nest in the reeds. In less than a mile you'll crest the hill and have a brief view of Petaluma before a steep descent to a residential street. Make your way through a new suburb to D Street, which has a wide shoulder for about 6 miles.

Petaluma built its reputation on the egg industry, but the dairy industry has outgrown it, accounting for $83 million of Sonoma County's revenue in 1999. Large ranches lie along Pt. Reyes–Petaluma Road. Traffic is moderate, and so are the hills on the way to a right turn on Hicks Valley Road. You can't miss the one-room Lincoln School, built in 1872, on this rarely traveled road. Its student population numbered twelve in 2000, and the students often teach each other.

After a gentle climb around Hammock Hill, you'll descend to the turnoff for Marshall-Petaluma Road, a narrow, two-lane country road heading west through the coastal hills, at least until the final ridge before Tomales Bay. The moderately steep climb rewards you with a bay view.

On Highway 1 you'll have to contend with increased traffic, although the winding road keeps speeds down. Traffic isn't heavy in

MILEAGE LOG

18

0.0 Start mileage from the yellow iron gate on a paved recreation path next to the restrooms. 0.8 Top of hill.

1.1 Left on Oxford Court where path ends.

1.2 Right on Windsor Drive at stop sign.

1.7 Right on D Street at stop sign, beginning climb. 2.5 Top of climb. 4.9 Marin County line. 6.1 Start climb. 7.4 Top of climb.

8.6 Right on Hicks Valley Road at green sign. 9.5 Start climb. 10.2 Top of climb.

11.3 Left on Marshall-Petaluma Road at T junction. 17.7 Start climb. 19.4 Top of climb.

22.2 Left on Highway 1 at stop sign. 27.6 Portable restroom at Keyes Creek fishing access.

29.0 Right on Tomales–Petaluma Road.

34.2 Right on Chileno Valley Road. 35.2 Start climb. 35.9 Top of climb.

43.7 Left at stop sign and T junction, staying on Chileno Valley Road.

46.7 End ride at Helen Putnam Regional Park.

---

the morning hours. This section of Highway 1 has the occasional bed and breakfast.

In Tomales you'll turn right and head inland on Tomales-Petaluma Road, a wide two-lane route popular with motorists heading to Highway 1 in the morning. After 5 miles, with a few climbs and descents, you'll turn right again onto Chileno Valley Road and once again find yourself alone with your thoughts. Few cars drive this road, but you will see bicyclists on weekends. Chileno Valley has everything you'd expect on a quiet Marin County road—a small lake, cows, oak-covered hills, and wildflowers in the spring.

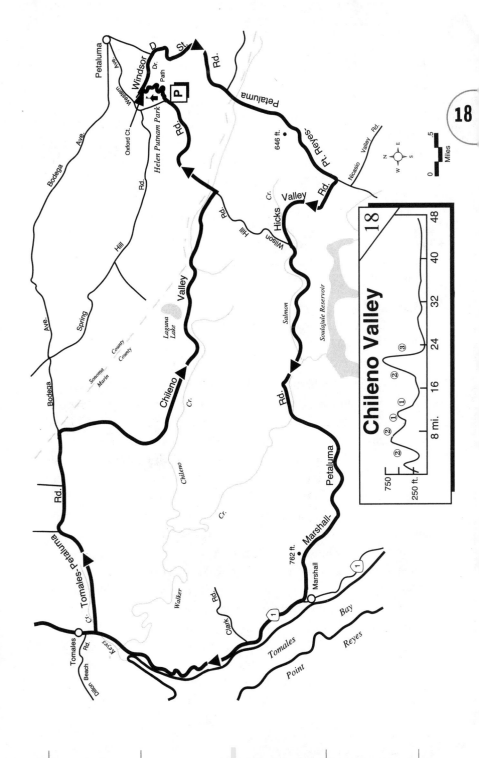

18

Chileno Valley

Napa Valley

IN ADDITION TO ITS FAMOUS VINE-yards and wineries, Napa Valley has some of the most interesting bike riding in Northern California. Fall may be the best season for touring the vineyards, with cool temperatures and traffic-free roads. On weekends, you'll often see colorful hot-air balloons over-head, and white gliders soaring on updrafts along the Palisades rock formation overlooking the town of Calistoga.

One of the best places to start a ride in Napa Valley is the town of St. Helena, centrally located for both bicycling and wine tasting. The short, flat ride loops through the valley, passing more than twenty wineries—Sutter Home, Louis Martini, Robert Mondavi, and Christian Brothers among them.

Start early to avoid the heat and traffic on Highway 29, the busiest road in the valley. Most wineries have tastings from 10 A.M. to 4 P.M. Train tracks crossing Highway 29 at two locations are probably the worst hazard you'll encounter. Because the tracks cross the road diag-onally, slow down and take them at right angles. The two-lane Silverado Trail carries much less traffic than Highway 29. It also offers better views, because it overlooks the valley in many places.

The long, hilly ride leaves the vineyards behind in pursuit of rural scenery and spectacular views of the valley. Along the way, you'll have numerous opportunities to stop and see interesting landmarks. Don't miss the Bale Grist Mill, now a state park. The giant wooden water-wheel measures 36 feet in diameter and weighs 5.5 tons. It was built in 1846 by Dr. Edward Bale. The flour mill closed in 1905; in 1974 the mill site became a state historic park, and restoration began in 1980.

On the way up Highway 29 you'll have impressive views of Napa Valley, the rocky red cliffs of the Palisades, and Sugarloaf Mountain. Instead of taking the highway all the way, try Old Stage Road (or Lawley Road). John Lawley built the narrow, bumpy road in 1874 as a toll road. Lawley, an early entrepreneur in Napa Valley, had good business sense when he built the road. It became the best route to Mt. St. Helena, which at the time was one giant mine shaft, with mining towns like Silverado clinging to its slopes.

When the railroad reached Calistoga in 1868, Lawley realized a properly graded road would speed deliveries to the mines. The alternate route, up Oat Hill Road, between Calistoga and Middletown, was even steeper than the route Lawley built. Three years after completing the road, Lawley built the Toll House, a family residence, inn, and horse stable at the road's summit. The original house burned down in 1883; a second house built at the same site burned down in 1951. In 1923 the state purchased the toll road and built Highway 29, although the upper highway still follows Lawley Road.

Two well-known figures associated with Mt. St. Helena were the writer Robert Louis Stevenson and the robber Black Bart. Stevenson wrote *Treasure Island*, *The Strange Case of Dr. Jekyll and Mr. Hyde*, and *Kidnapped*. In 1880 he lived on the mountain with his bride. Their residence turned to dust, but you can still visit the site in Robert Louis Stevenson Park by hiking in 1 mile from the Highway 29 summit parking lot.

Charles Boles, alias Black Bart, also frequented the hills above Calistoga, robbing—with an unloaded gun—Wells Fargo stagecoaches traveling the toll road. His eight-year crime spree lasted until 1883; he spent his remaining years in San Quentin prison.

You can't miss Hubcap Ranch on Pope Valley Road. The ranch has been declared a state historic landmark. Litto Diamonte, an Italian immigrant, moved to the valley to farm in the early 1900s. His hubcap collection, which started as a joke, grew into the thousands, until hubcaps covered the house and barn and lined the fences. Diamonte died in 1983, but his legacy shines on.

Pope Valley has a store where you can get food and drink before the final steep climb. It is closed on Saturdays, as are all stores in the

MILEAGE LOG
RIDE 1: VALLEY TOUR

0.0 Start mileage at intersection of Pope Street and Highway 29 and ride east on Pope. Parking available at nearby high school.

0.8 Right on Silverado Trail at stop sign after crossing stone bridge over Napa River. 5.3 ZD Winery on right.

7.3 Right on Oakville Cross Road.

9.8 Right on Highway 29 at stop sign. 11.8 BV Winery on right. Beware of train tracks on Highway 29. 12.2 Beware of train tracks. 14.4 Heitz Cellars Winery on right. 14.5 Louis Martini winery on right. 14.8 Christian Brothers winery on right.

15.6 End ride at start.

RIDE 2: MOUNTAIN TOUR

0.0 Start mileage at corner of Deer Park Road and Highway 29. Parking available in St. Helena. Ride north on Highway 29 to Calistoga. 1.7 Old Bale Grist Mill State Park. 3.4 Bothe–Napa Valley State Park.

6.8 Right on Lincoln Avenue at stop sign (Highway 29) to downtown Calistoga.

7.8 Keep left at Silverado Trail junction.

9.3 Right on Old Stage Road (also called Lawley Road). Begin steep 4.7-mile climb in 0.9 miles.

12.6 Right on Highway 29 at stop sign, continuing climb. 14.6 Summit. Robert Louis Stevenson State Park and hiking trail to Mt. St. Helena summit on left. 15.2 Unpaved service road to Mt. St. Helena summit, open to bicycles. 18.1 Lake County. 23.8 Downtown Middletown. Food and drink.

24.4 Right on Butts Canyon Road at cemetery. 29.0 Oat Hill Road junction on right. 29.7 Detert Reservoir. 35.5 Snell Valley Road junction on left. Butts Canyon Road becomes Pope Valley Road. Begin 1.1-mile climb. 36.6 Summit. Begin 1.3-mile descent to Pope Valley. 38.4 Bridge over Pope Creek. 40.6 Hubcap Ranch.

42.9 Right on Howell Mountain Road in Pope Valley at stop sign. Begin steep 2.3-mile climb. 45.2 Summit. 46.7 Straight at College Avenue junction. 47.0 Town of Angwin. 48.9 Howell Mountain Road changes name to Deer Park Road at four-way intersection. 52.8 Continue straight at stop sign for Silverado Trail.

53.5 End ride at start.

---

town of Angwin, which was built by Seventh-day Adventists. Near the end of the ride you'll get a chance to test your gears on Howell Mountain Road leading to Angwin. The 2-mile ascent has a grade of 9 to 13 percent.

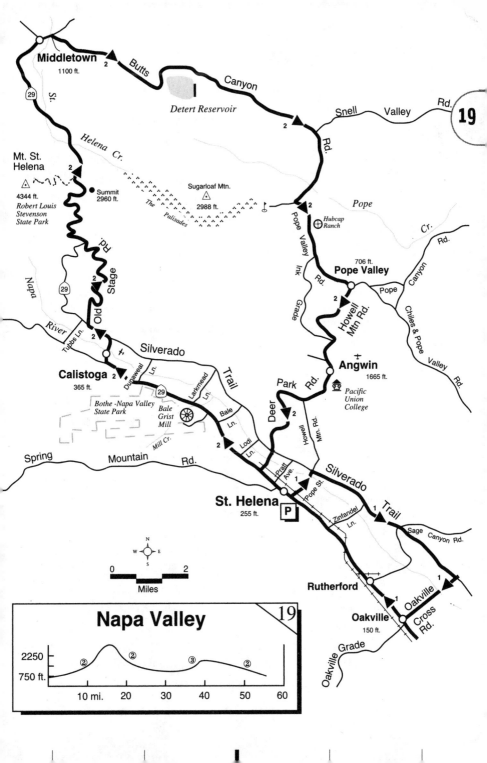

Marin Headlands

DISTANCE >>> 16 miles

TERRAIN >>> Hilly

TRAFFIC >>> Light

HOW TO GET THERE >>> From Interstate 280, take the Highway 1 Pacifica exit headed west. Go about a half-mile and then exit right on Skyline Boulevard. Turn left onto the Great Highway at a stop sign next to Lake Merced. Continue straight, following the road around the Cliff House. The road becomes Point Lobos Avenue and then Geary Boulevard. Left on 25th Avenue. At the stop sign, go right on Camino del Mar, which becomes Lincoln Boulevard. Continue to the top of the hill and then watch carefully for Merchant Road on the left, just before Lincoln descends. Park at Battery Boutelle a short distance off Lincoln Avenue. Coming from north of the Golden Gate Bridge, cross the bridge and exit at the first right after the toll plaza on Merchant Road.

REWARDING VIEWS—ONE AFTER another—make this hilly ride through the easily accessible Marin Headlands just north of San Francisco well worth the effort. In 1972, foresighted individuals preserved the scenic lands around the Golden Gate with the formation of the Golden Gate National Recreation Area (GGNRA).

Of course, no cyclist's life in and around San Francisco would be complete without riding over the Golden Gate Bridge, another enticement for riding to the Marin Headlands. The experience of riding on the sidewalk next to cars roaring by is hardly pleasurable, but once past the bridge you can take in its beauty from a distance.

Begin riding from a parking lot next to Battery Boutelle at the south end of the bridge, just west of the toll plaza. The concrete fortress was built in 1901 and decommissioned at the end of World War II. None of the guns overlooking the Golden Gate ever fired at an enemy.

For your safety, obey these rules when crossing the bridge: Ride on the west sidewalk on weekends and holidays, the east side on weekdays. It's illegal to do otherwise. Keep your speed down to 15 mph or

It's all downhill from here, looking north to Point Bonita.

less. Ride carefully, as it can be wet, cold, and windy at any time of year. Iron gratings on the sidewalk are slippery when wet. Use extreme caution when riding around the two towers. Follow signs from the parking lot to a path under the bridge. It's an uphill ride for the first half of the span's 1.7 miles.

People from around the world fêted the bridge's fiftieth birthday on May 25, 1987, with extravagant fireworks and the inauguration of permanent lighting for the span's twin towers. More than fifty thousand people—the heaviest load supported by the bridge—jammed onto the 8,940-foot span, which remained closed to traffic for six hours. The structure they were celebrating took six years to build, cost $35 million, and claimed the lives of eleven workers. It was the longest suspension bridge in the world at the time.

After you cross the bridge, there's a fairly steep climb up Conzelman Road, where you'll have uncompromised views of the Golden Gate Bridge when the ever-present fog burns off. From the top

MILEAGE LOG

20

0.0 Start ride at Battery Boutelle parking area on Merchant Road. There's plenty of parking in the dirt lot. Ride east on Merchant Road.

0.1 Left and downhill to subway under Golden Gate Bridge toll booth.

0.2 Left on other side of subway, up road with DO NOT ENTER sign (OK for bikes). Ride past circular gift shop. Road takes you to east bridge sidewalk for 10 yards. On weekends take the west sidewalk. Go right at the green bike sign. Ride 20 yards and make a U-turn to ride under the bridge on a paved path.

0.4 Left, entering the west bridge sidewalk.

2.1 Left through gap in fence into parking area and ride uphill to stop sign.

2.2 Left at stop sign onto Conzelman Road, beginning 1.9-mile climb. 2.5 Battery Spencer on left. Dirt road beyond Spencer open to bikes, goes to Kirby Cove.

3.4 Keep straight at junction with McCullough Road on right. 4.0 Summit, begin steep 0.8-mile descent on narrow one-way road.

5.9 Keep straight at junction, continuing to Point Bonita and circling around hill.

6.2 Right at stop sign onto Field Road. Battery Mendell visible to the west. 7.0 Marin Headlands Visitor Center. Restrooms. Youth Hostel uphill on right.

7.1 Left at sign for beach, followed by stop sign.

7.6 Keep straight at junction to Ft. Cronkhite. 8.1 Ride around iron gate and begin climb. 8.6 Battery Townsley on left.

8.8 Left at junction, go 20 yards, and then turn around to return back down the hill. Coastal Trail open to bikes here. 9.5 Ride around gate.

11.0 Keep straight at junction. Becomes Bunker Road.

12.3 Right on McCullough Road, beginning 0.9-mile climb.

13.2 Left on Conzelman Road at stop sign, beginning descent to Golden Gate Bridge.

14.3 Right into parking area at entrance to west sidewalk of Golden Gate Bridge. 14.4 Begin sidewalk.

16.1 Right off bridge and take path under bridge. Make a U-turn about 100 yards from end of sidewalk to reach the east sidewalk. Left on east sidewalk for about 10 yards, then downhill on road past the circular gift shop.

16.2 Right under toll plaza subway.

16.3 Left on other side of subway. Then right onto Merchant Road.

16.4 End ride.

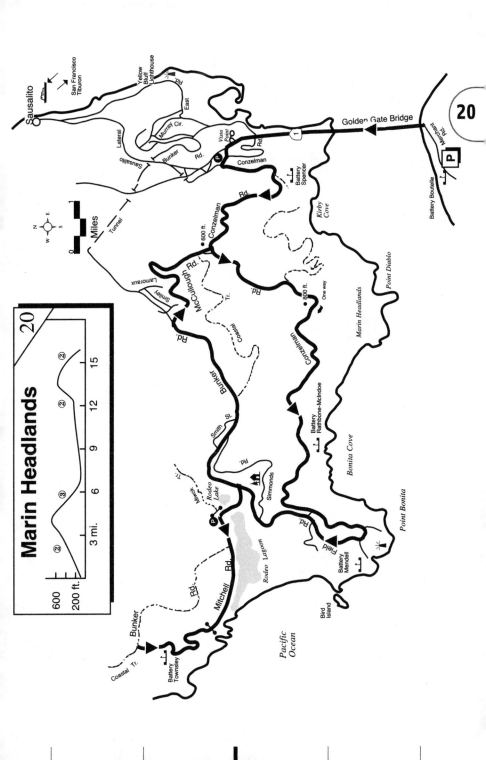

of the climb you can see San Francisco and the Pacific Ocean. Begin a steep descent on a one-way road, where the landscape in the early spring looks more like Ireland than California.

You'll ride past Rodeo Lagoon, a gathering place for surfers and hiking groups. For some more beautiful views of the Pacific, continue past the iron gate uphill on a fairly steep grade. On quiet days it's just you, the roar of the surf, crying seagulls, and ringing buoy bells.

Return the way you came, except that you'll ride through a valley on Bunker Road and then climb McCullough Road to Conzelman Road before descending to the Golden Gate Bridge.

Muir Woods

DISTANCE >>> 27 miles

TERRAIN >>> Two major climbs

TRAFFIC >>> Light to heavy

HOW TO GET THERE >>> From Highway 101 north, take the Highway 1 exit and immediately after exiting, turn right onto Pohono Street. There's a parking area next to Richardson Bay Bridge. From Highway 101 south, take the Highway 1 exit and circle right back under the freeway to get to Pohono Street.

MARIN COUNTY'S STATELY REDWOODS have attracted tourists by the millions for decades. On this ride, you'll visit the world-renowned Muir Woods National Monument and the rest of the best that Marin County offers.

The ride starts in Marin City at Richardson Bay and goes north through downtown Mill Valley. The town was settled by loggers in the 1840s, who found work at a sawmill on Old Mill Creek. By 1900, the logging industry had slowed and tourism took over. Mill Valley quickly became a playground for San Francisco's rich and famous, who delighted in riding the "Crookedest Railroad in the World" to the summit of Mt. Tamalpais. The woodsy town experienced another growth spurt in 1906, when refugees from the San Francisco earthquake and fire settled here. Today, the town at the base of Mt. Tamalpais has an eclectic population of writers, entertainers, and artists.

The route parallels the former right-of-way of the North Pacific Coast Railroad on Miller Avenue. The train depot, built in 1925, is located in Lytton Square; it's now a bookstore and coffee shop.

Leaving downtown Mill Valley, you'll pass the remnants of John Reed's sawmill in Old Mill Park. Continue northwest through the park to the winding, narrow Marion Avenue nestled in the redwoods. The concrete road climbs steadily past houses clinging to steep slopes. Turn right onto Edgewood Avenue, and stay left at the Sequoia Valley Road junction.

At Panoramic Highway, turn right and continue climbing on the two-lane road to the high point of the ride, at 1,500 feet. On hot

MILEAGE LOG

21

0.0 Start mileage at the parking area under the Richardson Bay Bridge in Marin City, right off Pohono Street. Ride north on a paved recreation path. 0.2 Cross bridge over Coyote Creek.

0.6 Left, leaving path, onto Miller Avenue at crosswalk, and then immediate right on Miller Avenue, which has a bike lane.

2.5 Left where Miller forks in front of the bookstore. Then turn right in 15 yards at a stop sign, continuing on Miller Avenue a short distance to Throckmorton Avenue. Left at the Throckmorton Avenue stop sign.

2.8 Left on Cascade Avenue into Old Mill Park. Keep right at the next junction.

3.1 Left on Marion Avenue, uphill on a concrete road.

4.1 Right on Edgewood Avenue at stop sign. Keep left on Sequoia Valley Road in 0.4 miles.

5.1 Right on Panoramic Highway at stop sign.

8.7 Left at Pantoll park headquarters, staying on Panoramic Highway to Highway 1.

13.3 Left on Highway 1 at stop sign.

19.2 Left on Muir Woods Road. 21.7 Muir Woods National Monument. Bicycles not allowed in park. Drinking fountains and restrooms found in parking area.

23.4 Right on Panoramic Highway at stop sign. Summit.

24.3 Left on Highway 1 at stop sign, continuing descent to bay.

26.8 Right at traffic light, staying on Highway 1. Ride about 200 yards, cross bridge and turn right on Tennessee Valley Road. Ride through gravel parking area on your right and walk or ride under bridge on a narrow path. Continue straight and pick up a paved recreation path beyond the bridge. If the path is blocked by high tide, stay on Highway 1 and return to start by riding under Richardson Bay Bridge.

27.2 Right at path junction.

27.4 End ride at parking area under bridge.

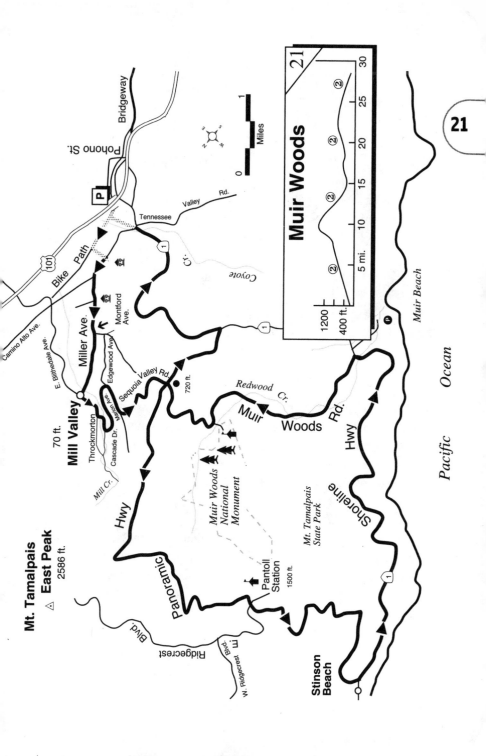

Mt. Tamalpais
△ East Peak
2586 ft.

Muir Woods

21

Pacific   Ocean

Muir Beach

Stinson Beach

Mill Valley
70 ft.

Muir Woods National Monument

Mt. Tamalpais State Park

1500 ft.

Pantoll Station

720 ft.

Redwood Cr.

Muir   Woods   Rd.

Shoreline

Panoramic   Hwy

Ridgecrest Blvd.

W. Ridgecrest Blvd.

Hwy

Throckmorton

Mill Cr.

Cascade Dr.

Marion Ave.

Sequoia Valley Rd.

Edgewood Ave.

Miller Ave.

Montford Ave.

E. Blithedale Ave.

Camino Alto Ave.

US 101

Bike   Path

Pohono St.

Bridgeway

Tennessee   Valley   Rd.

Coyote   Cr.

1

1

1

P

P

0   1
Miles

N W E S

1200
400 ft.

5 mi.   10   15   20   25   30

②   ②   ②   ②   ②

21

People flock to Stinson Beach on warm days.

days, the road is crowded with traffic going to Stinson Beach. Now that the climbing is over, you can have some fun riding down to the Coast Highway (Highway 1), where you'll turn left.

The Coast Highway between Stinson Beach and Muir Beach Overlook follows the rocky Pacific shoreline's towering cliffs before turning inland. The two-lane road, which was closed for extensive repairs in 1990–91, has no shoulder.

Turn left onto the quiet Muir Woods Road and ride up the wooded Frank Valley along Redwood Creek. The final climb starts at the entrance to Muir Woods National Monument.

Marin County's only remaining old-growth redwoods survived the ax thanks to William Kent. Kent's land faced condemnation by a water company intent on building a reservoir. Eventually, the legislator learned about a little-known law that turned valuable parcels into a national monument. Previous efforts to give the land to the government or have it declared a state park had failed.

In 1908, 295 acres were presented to the U.S. government and accepted by President Teddy Roosevelt. Kent asked that the monument be named after John Muir, who had campaigned to make Yosemite Valley a national park.

The twisty descent on busy Highway 1 begins at the Panoramic Highway junction. Follow a recreation path back to the parking area under Highway 101, as described in the Mileage Log.

Point Reyes

DISTANCE >>> 54 miles

TERRAIN >>> One long climb, several short climbs

TRAFFIC >>> Light to heavy

HOW TO GET THERE >>> From Highway 101, take the Sir Francis Drake Boulevard (San Anselmo) exit going west. Drive about 6 miles on a mostly two-lane road to downtown Fairfax. At the traffic light near the tall, blocky Fairfax Theater sign, turn left. There's parking next to Broadway.

MARIN COUNTY PROBABLY HAS ONE of the highest concentrations of bicyclists anywhere in the United States. Point Reyes brings out the bike riders. The peninsula is one giant park—federal, state, county, city, and public water district. Without this kind of protection, Marin County might be Condo County.

Fairfax, last in a string of towns on Sir Francis Drake Boulevard, has parking at the beginning of Bolinas Avenue between Sir Francis Drake and Broadway. A block east on Broadway, look for the Fairfax Theater.

Bolinas Avenue becomes Fairfax Bolinas Road at San Anselmo Creek. Houses perched on wooden columns cling to a canyon covered with toyon, bay laurel, poison oak, redwoods, and oaks. A mile from the summit you'll pass the Meadow Club Golf Course. The Marin water district maintains the gate on the road next to the golf course. It closes the road on days when fire danger is high. Call (415) 924-4600 to check on the road's status.

Look for Alpine Lake far below from the first of two ridgetops. Pine Mountain Road on the right has been used in the past for the Thanksgiving Day mountain bike ride starting in Fairfax. As you look at the forested hillsides, note that this is all Marin County watershed. After an invigorating descent on the two-lane road, you'll wind through the redwoods to Alpine Lake dam, built in 1919.

The road climbs steadily through redwoods and Douglas fir from the dam to Bolinas Ridge. Turn right at the summit. Bolinas Ridge Trail

MILEAGE LOG

0.0 Start mileage in Fairfax at the parking lot between Sir Francis Drake Boulevard and Broadway, near the junction with Fairfax Bolinas Road. Ride south on Bolinas Avenue (name changes to Fairfax Bolinas Road). 2.5 Meadow Club Golf Course. 3.7 Summit. 8.0 Cross Alpine Dam.

10.3 Right at summit and stop sign for West Ridgecrest Boulevard junction. Fairfax Bolinas Road continues to right.

14.6 Right on Highway 1 at stop sign. 15.2 Dogtown. 23.7 Olema.

23.8 Left on Bear Valley Road.

24.7 Left to Point Reyes National Seashore Park Headquarters. Return to Bear Valley Road and turn left.

26.7 Left on Sir Francis Drake Boulevard at stop sign. 27.2 Inverness Park.

29.8 Inverness. Return on Sir Francis Drake Boulevard to Highway 1, keeping left at the Bear Valley Road junction.

33.4 Left on Highway 1 at stop sign. 34.0 Ride through Point Reyes Station on Highway 1.

34.4 Right on Point Reyes Petaluma Road.

37.9 Right on Platform Bridge Road at stop sign.

40.2 Right at bike route sign just before Sir Francis Drake Boulevard stop sign. Cross bridge over Lagunitas Creek.

40.3 Left onto Cross Marin recreation path. 42.5 Taylorville paper mill site.

43.5 Left over bridge to leave Samuel P. Taylor State Park at main entrance.

43.7 Right on Sir Francis Drake Boulevard at stop sign.

54.0 Fairfax. End ride.

---

on your right is described in the Bolinas Ridge ride. Begin the descent to Highway 1. Poorly banked, bumpy corners will test your riding skills.

Highway 1 runs down the middle of the San Andreas Valley, rolling over short hills, through groves of eucalyptus and green pastures. If it hasn't been stolen, you might see the Dogtown sign (population 30), bolted to a eucalyptus tree.

The town of Olema has stores where you can stop for a snack. You're only a mile away from the Point Reyes National Seashore headquarters, which has a spacious interpretive center, restrooms, and drinking fountains.

The park was established in 1962, when about 64,000 acres were purchased; ranchers still lease Point Reyes land for cattle grazing. Point Reyes used to be part of Southern California, until it broke away and drifted slowly north over the past 100 million years or so. As Point

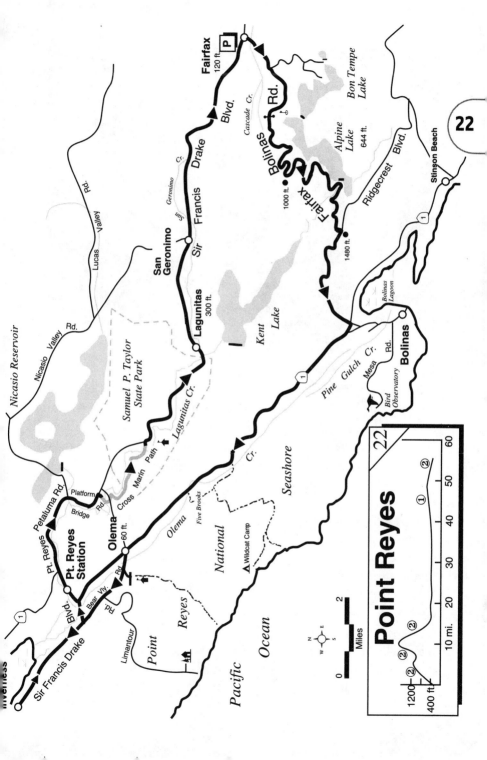

Inverness

Sir Francis Drake

Pt. Reyes

Petaluma Rd.

Nicasio Valley Rd.

Nicasio Reservoir

Lucas Valley Rd.

Platform

Bridge

Marin

Path

Cross

Rd.

Samuel P. Taylor State Park

Lagunitas Cr.

San Geronimo

Sir Francis Drake

San Geronimo Cr.

Cascade Cr.

Fairfax 120 ft.

P

Bolinas Rd.

Bon Tempe Lake

Alpine Lake 644 ft.

Fairfax Bolinas Rd.

1000 ft.

1480 ft.

Ridgecrest Blvd.

Stinson Beach

Lagunitas 300 ft.

Kent Lake

1

Bird Observatory

Bolinas

Mesa Rd.

Pine Gulch Cr.

Bolinas Lagoon

Bear Vly. Rd.

Limantour Rd.

Pt. Reyes Station

Blvd.

Olema 60 ft.

Olema Cr.

Five Brooks

Wildcat Camp

Point

Reyes

National

Seashore

Pacific Ocean

1

N
W   E
S

0   Miles   2

Point Reyes

22

1200
400 ft
10 mi.   20   30   40   50   60
② ②②   ②   ①   ②

Fairfax Bolinas Road winds around Alpine Lake.

Reyes continues its slow drift on the continental plate, it will reach Oregon in 50 million years, give or take a few million.

Exit park headquarters and head north to Inverness. On the way back, you'll visit Point Reyes Station before picking up Point Reyes Petaluma Road about a half-mile outside town. Platform Bridge Road follows Lagunitas Creek to Sir Francis Drake Boulevard.

Cross an old bridge over the creek before the stop sign, and immediately turn left onto the Cross Marin recreation path, which leads into Samuel P. Taylor State Park. The path was a right-of-way for the North Pacific Coast Railroad. It follows Lagunitas Creek under an umbrella of trees. You'll see a historical marker with details about the site of the first paper mill west of the Mississippi. The mill was built by Samuel Taylor in 1856. Taylorville, a company town and health resort, sprang up along the banks of Lagunitas Creek.

Leave the park through the main entrance and cross a bridge over the creek. You're back on Sir Francis Drake Boulevard, which passes through the towns of Lagunitas, Forest Knolls, and San Geronimo on the return to Fairfax.

Clayton

DISTANCE >>> 53 miles

TERRAIN >>> Moderately hilly

TRAFFIC >>> Mostly light; heavy in Walnut Creek

HOW TO GET THERE >>> From Interstate 680, take the Diablo Road exit west and drive about a half-mile to Hartz Avenue. Turn left at the traffic light, and it's less than a half-mile to Church Street on the right.

THIS RIDE CIRCLES THE VOLCANO-shaped Mt. Diablo, so you'll have stunning views of its steep, rocky eastern slope. Adding to the enjoyment will be a memorable climb on the secluded Morgan Territory Road.

Start at the base of Mt. Diablo in the town of Danville, off Interstate 680. Danville was a farm community until the 1950s, when improved water service brought rapid growth. The town was named for the first settlers to the area, brothers Daniel and Andrew Inman, who arrived in 1852. Some of the town's history is preserved at the Southern Pacific train depot on Railroad Avenue, near where the ride begins. The newly refurbished wooden building is reminiscent of the simpler days of the iron horse.

Ride northwest on Hartz Avenue from the California Pedaler bike shop. The road to Walnut Creek has a wide shoulder and bike lanes, with moderate to light traffic. Danville Road follows a former stage-coach route between Martinez and San Jose, passing century-old ranches and acres of walnut orchards. In late winter, yellow mustard carpets the orchards. Wheat was grown here in the late 1880s, to be replaced by vineyards and orchards.

The mood and scenery changes in Walnut Creek, where traffic is heavy most weekdays and even on weekends. The modern city's glass-and-steel buildings dwarf the older brick structures you'll see on Main Street.

In contrast to the busy streets of downtown Walnut Creek, Contra Costa Canal shines like a recreational gem. A paved path follows the canal into woodsy neighborhoods. Watch out for pedestrians, in-line

MILEAGE LOG

0.0 Start mileage at the intersection of Church Street and South Hartz Avenue, next to California Pedaler bike shop, 495 South Hartz Avenue; phone (925) 820-0345. Ride north on South Hartz Avenue, which becomes North Hartz and then Danville Boulevard. 5.0 Walnut Creek city limits sign. 5.5 Interstate 680 overpass. 5.9 Main Street.

6.7 Right on Civic Drive at traffic light.

8.2 Right on Contra Costa Canal recreation trail. Watch for the yellow road sign that says "Trail Crossing."

Morgan Territory Road rises to 2,000 feet, where there's a spectacular view of San Ramon Valley.

11.3 Left at junction over Contra Costa Canal bridge.

11.7 Right on Treat Boulevard.

13.5 Right on Clayton Road at traffic light.

17.1 Right on Marsh Creek Road at traffic light.

18.1 Keep right on Marsh Creek Road at second traffic light. 19.6 Rodie's Store. Last chance for food or drink until Danville.

21.5 Right on Morgan Territory Road. In 4 miles road narrows. 30.7 Morgan Territory Regional Preserve parking area on left. Restrooms, hiking, off-road riding available. 31.0 Summit. Begin descent to Manning Road.

36.1 Right on Manning Road at stop sign.

37.0 Right on Highland Road at stop sign.

41.7 Right on Camino Tassajara at stop sign.

43.0 Right on Finley Road. 43.6 Old Tassajara School. Return.

44.2 Right on Camino Tassajara at stop sign.

50.3 Left on Sycamore Valley Road at Camino Tassajara junction.

51.8 Right on San Ramon Valley Boulevard at stop light, just after crossing Interstate 680 overpass. Becomes North Hartz Avenue.

52.5 End ride at Church Street.

skaters, and other cyclists using the path, and use caution crossing busy streets. You'll leave the canal at Treat Boulevard and ride south on Clayton Road, a wide avenue lined with retail stores.

Though urban sprawl has slowed considerably in the Bay Area, a final bastion in what was once a rural setting has fallen—Clayton. Leaving shopping centers, Clayton Road drops you into the town center. Joel Clayton, a San Francisco dairyman, founded the town. Coal and copper mines in the nearby hills gave residents a modest livelihood until the late 1800s, when vineyards and wineries sprang up. A few old buildings have been preserved, but Clayton is surrounded by subdivisions.

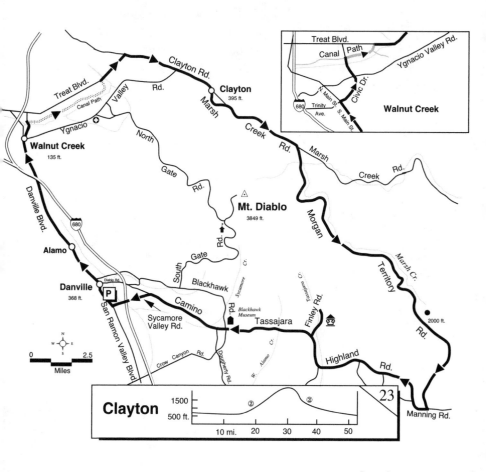

The walnut trees outside this one-room school on Finley Road were planted by students in the early 1900s.

Outside Clayton, the rocky spire of Mt. Diablo's eastern face reveals itself. Legend has it that local resident Jeremiah Morgan "discovered" this rugged area in 1856 while hunting on Mt. Diablo. As he looked out over the hills, he declared all the land in view to be his, about 10,000 acres' worth.

Turn right on Morgan Territory Road, where you'll enter a wide valley that soon narrows. The road snakes uphill, following Marsh Creek under a canopy of oaks. It's a steady climb to 2,000 feet, with only a couple of short, steep pitches. At the summit you're rewarded with a spectacular view of ranch lands to the west and south. After a brisk descent to Manning Road, the ride turns mostly flat to Danville. Don't miss Tassajara School on Finley Road. Rows of majestic walnut trees, planted by students in 1904, give welcome shade to the one-room schoolhouse. The bell tower and turnstile were common features for schools built in 1888.

Return to Danville on Camino Tassajara Road, which passes "executive homes" in the Blackhawk development. Farther along, near the junction with Blackhawk Road, Blackhawk Museum is worth a visit. It's located in the Shops at Blackhawk, in the northeast corner. The car museum includes a rare Tucker 1948 Torpedo.

East Bay Reservoirs

AFTER RIDING THROUGH THE CROWDED streets of Berkeley and Oakland, the wide-open spaces of the East Bay watershed bring welcome relief. The original Rancho El Sobrante land grant has turned into a veritable "Rancho La Bicicleta." Hundreds of riders tour the open spaces on fair-weather weekends.

The watershed's lands were purchased from Mexico in 1841 by Victor and Juan Castro. (*Sobrante* is Spanish for "vacant" or "remaining.") Squatters quickly moved onto the Castro property, and before long the land was parceled out. In 1868, a son of one of the Castros built a ranch at the intersection of Castro Ranch Road and San Pablo Dam Road.

Start the ride in downtown Orinda, loop around the Briones and San Pablo dams, and return to town. As you ride under the busy Highway 24 overpass, imagine what life was like here in 1941, when this intersection had the distinction of acquiring the first traffic light in the area. San Pablo Dam Road wasn't paved until 1919. In 1952, it was widened and straightened to its present alignment. The only evidence of a building boom in the valley comes on Castro Ranch Road, where subdivisions line the hillside at the top of a short climb. In contrast, the ranches and hay fields in Alhambra Valley still see little traffic.

A challenging climb greets you on Bear Creek Road. On hot summer days plan your ride accordingly. Bear Creek Road rolls up and down on the way to Alhambra Valley Road, with two major but gradual climbs.

The watershed's dams were built during World War I. As early as the 1890s, local residents envisioned a dam on San Pablo Creek for

MILEAGE LOG

24

0.0 Start mileage at Highway 24 overpass, west branch. If driving, park in Orinda, or take BART to Orinda. Ride northwest on Camino Pablo.

2.4 Right on Bear Creek Road at traffic light. Two climbs to Briones Regional Park. 6.8 Briones Regional Park entrance on right. Two climbs to Alhambra Valley Road.

11.0 Left on Alhambra Valley Road at stop sign.

13.7 Left on Castro Ranch Road.

16.0 Left on San Pablo Dam Road at traffic light. 21.4 Bear Creek Road junction.

21.6 Ride under Highway 24. End ride.

---

irrigation. Construction began in 1916 and took three years using horse-drawn scrapers. San Pablo Dam was drained and reinforced in 1979 for $15 million to meet state earthquake standards.

The reservoir contains water from the creek and the Sierra Nevada. After a disastrous drought in 1918, a pipeline was built from the Mokelumne River in the Sierra Nevada. The East Bay Municipal Utility District project was completed in 1929, just in time to avert another water shortage.

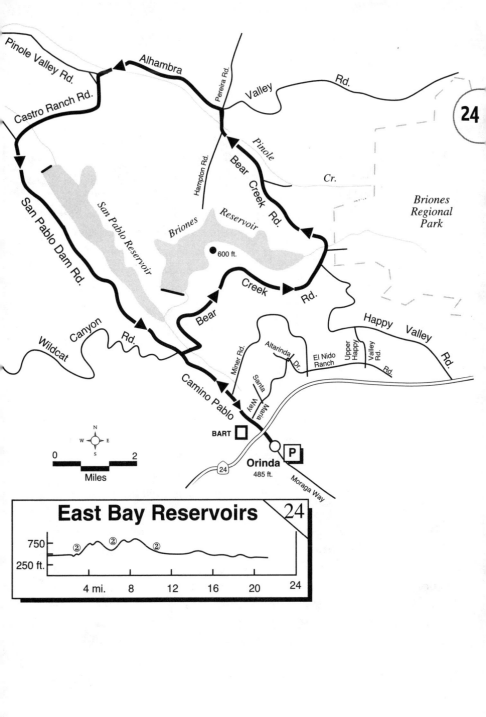

Pinole Valley Rd.

Alhambra

Pereira Rd.

Valley

Rd.

24

Castro Ranch Rd.

Pinole

Bear Creek Rd.

Cr.

Hampton Rd.

Briones Regional Park

San Pablo Reservoir

Briones Reservoir

600 ft.

San Pablo Dam Rd.

Creek

Rd.

Bear

Happy

Valley

Wildcat

Canyon

Rd.

Miner Rd.

Altarinda Dr.

El Nido Ranch

Upper Happy

Valley Rd.

Rd.

Camino Pablo

Santa Maria Way

N
W   E
S

0   2

Miles

BART

Orinda
485 ft.

P

24

Moraga Way

East Bay Reservoirs

24

750

250 ft.

② ② ②

4 mi.   8   12   16   20   24

Martinez

DISTANCE >>> 18 miles

TERRAIN >>> A few gentle hills

TRAFFIC >>> Light

HOW TO GET THERE >>> From Interstate 80, take the Highway 4 exit east. It's about 10 miles to Martinez. Exit at Alhambra Avenue, turning left at ramp. Cross beneath highway; John Muir House is immediately on your left. From Interstate 680 northbound, take Highway 4 westbound. Exit at Alhambra Avenue. Turn right at bottom of ramp. John Muir House is immediately on your left.

CARQUINEZ BRIDGE (WESTBOUND), spanning the Carquinez Strait, reflected the latest in bridge technology when it was built in 1927. The eastbound span was added in 1958. Their impressive steel girders resemble giant Erector sets. On this ride, you will see the bridges and experience the rural atmosphere of the Martinez-Crockett area.

The original Carquinez Bridge will be torn down and replaced with a new cantilever-style bridge around 2004. It will have a multiuse path accessible by bicycle. The span built in 1958 will be earthquake retrofitted.

Begin the ride in Martinez at the John Muir House, a national historic site maintained by the National Park Service. Muir, who was one of California's first and foremost environmentalists and a cofounder of the Sierra Club, lived here in his last years. He's buried in the cemetery you'll ride past as you enter Martinez. The house was built in 1882 by his father-in-law, John Strentzel. Muir moved into the house in 1890 and lived there until his death in 1914.

The park grounds have many varieties of plant life, as well as orchards and a vineyard. Don't miss the Martinez adobe in the rear of the estate. Don Vincente Martinez, son of the *commandante* of the Presidio of San Francisco, built the house of adobe bricks around 1848. It's the oldest dwelling in the area and a fine example of adobe construction.

The 18-mile ride goes through Alhambra Valley and along the shores of Carquinez Strait. There's a gradual climb on Franklin Canyon

Carquinez Bridge comes into view on the Crockett Boulevard descent.

Road, a quiet two-lane road following Highway 24. Beyond the summit, after crossing Highway 4, there's a fast, straight downhill on Crockett Boulevard.

On Carquinez Scenic Drive, you'll have the road to yourself; it was closed to cars by landslides in the 1970s and remains open only for bicycling and hiking. Short sections of road are unpaved. In the summer months, the brown hills offer a colorful contrast to the blue waters of Carquinez Strait. On the narrow shoreline, a rail line sees frequent use.

MILEAGE LOG

0.0 Start mileage at John Muir House.

0.1 Right on Franklin Canyon Road.
3.0 Begin gradual climb. 3.7 McEwen
Road at right

4.5 Right on Cummings Skyway at stop
sign. 6.0 Summit.

6.6 Right on Crockett Boulevard,
beginning descent.

8.6 Right at stop sign on Pomona Street.
Becomes Carquinez Scenic Drive.
Begin 0.6-mile climb. 10.3 Bull
Valley Staging Area for Carquinez
Strait shoreline.

11.4 Keep straight at three-way junction.
Steep hill on right goes to Highway 4.
12.5 Gate. Road closed past this
point. You may need to walk short
sections of the trail where the road
has fallen away. Rock crushing
yard on left. 13.3 Gate. 14.2 Gate.
16.0 John Nejedly Staging Area.
16.4 Carquinez Scenic Drive becomes
Talbart Street. Talbart Street turns left
in residential area.

16.5 Right on Berrellessa Street at stop
sign. One-way. 17.3 Becomes
Alhambra Valley Road.

18.3 End ride at John Muir House.

Even though it's at the fringe of the sprawling East Bay, Martinez retains its small-town charm. Its narrow, hilly streets next to the bay resemble those of San Francisco. In 1900, the town was a commercial transportation hub, serviced by a nearby ferry and a stagecoach. The well-known Alhambra Water Company started bottling water here in 1903.

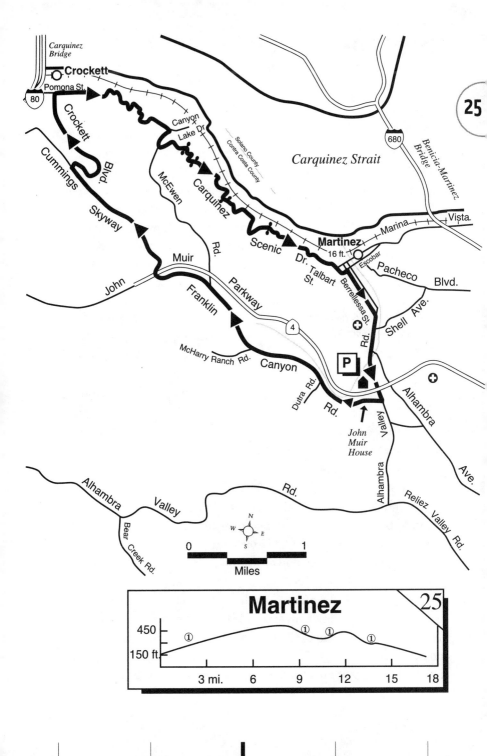

Mt. Diablo

DISTANCE >>> 29 miles

TERRAIN >>> Hilly

TRAFFIC >>> Light to moderate

HOW TO GET THERE >>> From Interstate 680, take the Diablo Road exit and go about a half-mile to Hartz Avenue. From the south, turn left after exiting and drive back under 680. Turn left on Hartz Avenue at the traffic light and drive south a short distance. Look for Church Street on the right. Parking is available on city streets and behind the railroad museum at Railroad Avenue and Prospect Avenue.

BICYCLISTS HAVE BEEN RIDING UP Mt. Diablo to the 3,489-foot summit ever since a toll road was built in 1879. Today, thousands of cyclists make the trip up, and there's an occasional race. There's nothing more satisfying than reaching the summit and taking in the view. On a clear day you can see the Farallon Islands, Mt. Shasta, the Sierra, and Monterey Bay.

Our love affair with the mountain dates back to the late 1800s, when the Mt. Diablo Summit Road Company built a sixteen-room hotel 3 miles from the summit. One of the builders, R. N. Burgess, was no stranger to mountain chalets; he had previously owned a hotel on 6,000-foot Mt. Washington in New Hampshire.

In 1891 the summit observation platform burned, and the hotel burned down a short time later. The toll road was closed and didn't reopen until 1915. In 1921 officials dedicated a parcel of land on Mt. Diablo to become a state park, and over the years the park has been expanded to include more than 15,000 acres.

You'll start riding from downtown Danville and take the south summit road, one of two approach roads into the park. The north and south approach roads join 4.6 miles from the summit at a ranger station.

After riding through several miles of urban setting, turn left at the south park entrance, identifiable by two small stone columns and an unobtrusive sign. The road snakes up the side of the mountain at a steady grade of about 6 percent. In spring the pleasant aroma of

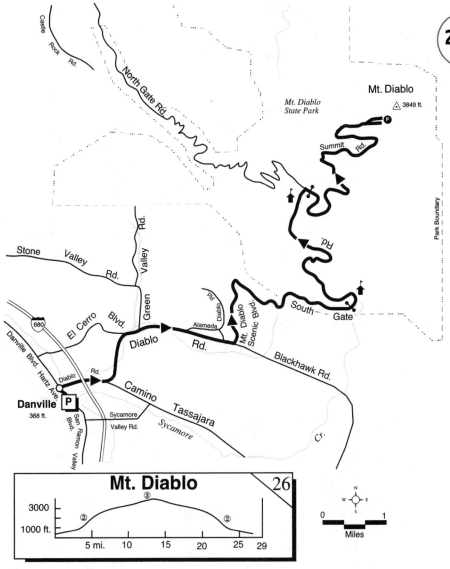

Castle
Rock Rd.

North Gate Rd.

Mt. Diablo
State Park

Mt. Diablo
△ 3849 ft.

Summit Rd.

Park Boundary

Stone Valley Rd.

Valley Rd.

Green

El Cerro Blvd.

Blvd.

Diablo Rd.

Diablo Rd.

Alameda

Mt. Diablo Scenic Blvd.

South Gate

Blackhawk Rd.

680

Danville Blvd. Hartz Ave.

Diablo Rd.

Danville
368 ft.

P

San Ramon Valley Blvd.

Camino Tassajara

Sycamore Valley Rd.

Sycamore

Cr.

Mt. Diablo
26

3000

1000 ft.

③

②

②

5 mi.   10   15   20   25   29

N
W ✦ E
S

0 ———————— 1
Miles

MILEAGE LOG

0.0 Start mileage in Danville on corner of Church Street and South Hartz Avenue next to California Pedaler bike shop at 495 South Hartz Avenue; phone (925) 820-0345. Ride north on South Hartz Avenue, which becomes North Hartz Avenue.

0.2 Right on Diablo Road at traffic light. 0.5 Interstate 680 underpass.

0.8 Keep left on Diablo Road at Camino Tassajara junction.

1.3 Right at traffic light, continuing on Diablo Road.

1.9 Keep right on Diablo Road at Green Valley Road junction. Diablo Road name changes to Blackhawk Road.

3.4 Left on Mt. Diablo Scenic Boulevard. Look for green sign and two stone columns. Name changes to South Gate Road. 7.4 South Gate park entrance.

9.7 Right on Summit Road at ranger station. 14.3 Summit. Return same route.

28.6 End ride.

---

buckbrush permeates the fresh, cool air. Park maps are available at the gate. Bicyclists enter for free.

Notice the rock outcropping, called Fossil Ridge, near the south-entrance ranger station. The sedimentary rock was pushed up with the rest of Mt. Diablo millions of years ago, exposing the fossilized remains of shellfish, mastadons, and saber-toothed tigers.

Turn right at the ranger station junction. The road steepens from here. You'll see Livermore Valley and Mt. Hamilton to the east and south. Just before reaching the summit, there's a parking lot on the right where the road branches. Keep right on the narrow one-way road that steepens to a breathtaking 18 percent for the next 300 yards. Return the way you came, but take the other one-way road leaving the parking lot.

It gets hot on Mt. Diablo in the summer, so start your ride early. Drinking fountains are located at the south ranger station and the main park office at the junction. Many campsites along the road have rest-rooms. There's a drinking fountain and a restroom at the summit, but the food stand inside the stone building shut down long ago.

Skyline Boulevard

DISTANCE >>> 28 miles

TERRAIN >>> Hilly

TRAFFIC >>> Light to moderate

HOW TO GET THERE >>> From Interstate 580, take Highway 24 east, drive through the Caldecott Tunnel, and then take the immediate right exit to Fish Ranch Road. Drive uphill. Turn right on Grizzly Peak Boulevard, then right on South Park Drive. This becomes Wildcat Canyon Road, which you stay on to the Inspiration Point parking lot. From the Berkeley BART station ride north on Spruce Street, which becomes Wildcat Canyon Road.

IF ASKED TO IDENTIFY THE MOST scenic ride in the Bay Area, the Oakland hills would be near the top of my list. There's no better vantage point for seeing San Francisco Bay, its bridges, and San Francisco. During the ups and downs on this hilly ride, you'll see redwood groves and elegant rural communities, as well. Fortunately, the scars from a devastating fire on October 20, 1991, are slowly receding.

The aptly named Inspiration Point in Tilden Regional Park offers a convenient location to start this tour. Go left from the parking lot, and descend the twisty two-lane Wildcat Canyon Road. Turn right at the bottom of the hill on Camino Pablo, and continue through Orinda to the town of Moraga. Traffic can be moderate to heavy, but the two-lane road has a wide shoulder and gentle climbs and descents. Moraga Way follows a railroad right-of-way dating back to 1889. The California and Nevada line was derailed by financial troubles, however, and never reached the town.

The town of Orinda, at the intersection of Camino Pablo and Highway 24, has a BART station. The intersection was formerly called The Crossroads because two of the region's oldest main roads crossed here.

Ranchers settled Moraga Valley in the 1870s. Moraga was named for Joaquin Moraga, an early valley settler in 1835 who received one of many large land grants from the Mexican government. The completion of the California and Nevada rail line between Berkeley and Orinda brought more settlers in 1890. In 1903, Orinda became even less

MILEAGE LOG

0.0 Start mileage at Inspiration Point in Tilden Regional Park at the summit of Wildcat Canyon Road. No services here. Turn left from parking lot and begin 2-mile descent.

2.4 Right on Camino Pablo Road at traffic light. 4.5 Ride under Highway 24 overpass. Camino Pablo becomes Moraga Way. 4.6 Downtown Orinda on left at Brookwood Road.

9.2 Right on Canyon Road at traffic light.

11.0 Left at Pinehurst Road junction and stop sign, beginning climb. Right goes steeply uphill to Skyline Boulevard. 12.2 Alameda County line. 12.5 Summit. Begin 1.2-mile descent.

13.7 Right on Redwood Road at stop sign. Begin 4-mile climb.

16.1 Right on Skyline Boulevard at traffic light.

16.7 Keep right on Skyline Boulevard at junction with Joaquin Miller Road. 17.7 Summit.

19.4 Keep right at junction with Carlsbrook Drive. 19.8 Drinking fountain on right at parking lot for Skyline Gate staging area in Redwood Regional Park.

20.2 Shallow left at Pinehurst Road junction, staying on Skyline.

20.8 Keep right at Snake Road junction. Begin 1.3-mile climb. 21.7 Drinking fountain on right at Robert Sibley park entrance.

21.8 Right on Grizzly Peak Road. 22.1 Summit. Road levels. Cross over Caldecott Tunnel. 22.4 View of Bay Area on left. 23.5 View. 24.0 Begin 0.2-mile descent.

24.2 Keep straight on Grizzly Peak Road at four-way stop. Begin 1.4-mile climb. 25.4 Steam train park on right. Drinking fountain at entrance.

25.6 Right on South Park Road, crossing train tunnel. Begin 1.5-mile descent.

27.1 Right on Wildcat Canyon Road at stop sign. Botanical Gardens straight ahead. Begin 1.2-mile climb.

28.3 End ride at Inspiration Point.

---

isolated from Oakland when tunnelers completed a road through the East Bay hills, just south of the Caldecott Tunnel. The old tunnel was closed in 1937 when Caldecott opened.

Continue on Moraga Way and turn right onto the lightly traveled Canyon Road. The shopping center at the intersection was built by developer Donald Rheem in 1950. Canyon Road climbs gradually through open hillsides and a grove of eucalyptus before descending to Pinehurst Road, where you're likely to experience a cool ride through the redwoods. The oldest and largest redwoods in the East Bay hills

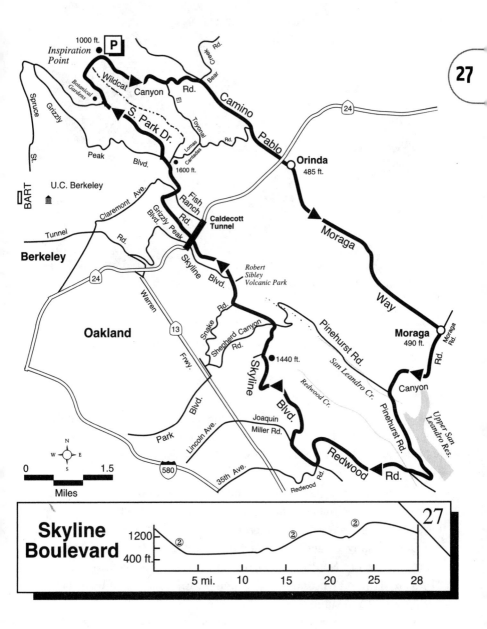

27

1000 ft. **P**
Inspiration Point

Botanical Gardens

Wildcat
Canyon   Rd.

Bear   Creek   Rd.

S. Park Dr.

El Toyonal

Lomas Centadas   Rd.

Camino   Pablo

Grizzly
Peak   Blvd.

1600 ft.

Orinda
485 ft.

24

BART

U.C. Berkeley

Claremont   Ave.

Tunnel   Rd.

Fish
Ranch
Rd.

**Caldecott
Tunnel**

Grizzly Peak Blvd.

Skyline   Blvd.

*Robert
Sibley
Volcanic Park*

Moraga   Way

Berkeley

24

Warren

13 Frwy.

Oakland

Snake   Rd.

Shepherd Canyon
Rd.

Skyline

1440 ft.

Pinehurst Rd.

San Leandro Cr.

Redwood Cr.

Moraga
490 ft.

Moraga   Rd.

Canyon

Skyline
Blvd.

Park   Blvd.

Lincoln Ave.

Joaquin
Miller Rd.

Pinehurst Rd.

Upper San Leandro Res.

N
W   E
S

0   1.5
Miles

580

35th. Ave.

Redwood   Rd.

Redwood Rd.

Canyon

**Skyline
Boulevard**

1200
400 ft.

② ② ②

5 mi.   10   15   20   25   28

27

Tilden Regional Park's miniature train attracts riders of all ages.

were logged here from 1840 to 1860. The ride can be shortened by turning right on Pinehurst Road, which passes through the "village" of Canyon, a former logging camp.

Turn left on Pinehurst and begin climbing. You'll soon see Upper San Leandro Reservoir, built in 1926. Turn right at Redwood Road. Food and drink are sold at Redwood Lodge, a rustic store about a mile from the junction. Turn right, staying on Skyline Boulevard, and climb another half-mile before turning right again on Skyline, at the Joaquin Miller Road junction.

Skyline rolls along the ridge of the East Bay hills between housing developments and regional parks. After passing Robert Sibley Volcanic Park, don't miss a key right turn onto Grizzly Peak Boulevard.

One of many attractions in the East Bay hills is a miniature steam train, just before South Park Drive. Train rides can be taken from 11 A.M. to 6 P.M. on weekends year-round, 12 P.M. to 5 P.M. on weekdays during spring and summer school vacations.

A quarter-mile past the train, turn right and begin a steep descent on South Park Drive. If you're taking this ride between November and March, the road will be closed to all but bicycles. Turn right at Wildcat

Canyon Road and ride back to Inspiration Point. In 1992, the East Bay Regional Park District started closing South Park Drive to cars during the winter to keep newts from being squashed. These slow-moving brownish-red salamanders cross the road to reach their mating grounds.

Near the end of the ride you'll pass the Botanical Gardens. The park replicates California's diverse vegetation and contains almost every plant native to the state. Hours are 10 A.M. to 5 P.M.

One way to celebrate the finish is to have a picnic at Inspiration Point. Walk or ride north on Nimitz Way, where you can watch the sun set behind the Golden Gate Bridge from the peaceful vantage point of a Nike missile bunker.

27

Sunol

28

DISTANCE >>> 28 miles

TERRAIN >>> Several gradual hills

TRAFFIC >>> Light to moderate

HOW TO GET THERE >>> From Interstate 680 northbound, take the Niles Canyon Road/Calaveras Road exit. Turn left at the stop sign, drive under 680 and continue west about a mile to reach Sunol. Turn right right after crossing the creek. From 680 southbound take the Highway 84/Sunol exit and then go right to Sunol after about a mile.

YOU MIGHT CALL THIS EAST BAY TOUR the "Ride of Three Canyons"— Niles, Stonybrook, and Dublin. You'll loop through scenic countryside, passing famous rail lines, two local wineries, and the western edge of Amador Valley.

Start the tour in Sunol, a rural town near Niles Canyon Road (Highway 84) and Interstate 680. Sunol's residents have an easygoing sense of humor. At one time their honorary mayor was Bosco, a 70-pound Labrador retriever who occasionally wandered off for weeks at a time.

Sunol may make light of its mayor, but it takes its trains seriously. It's home to the Niles Canyon Scenic Railroad, a collection of steam locomotives owned by the Pacific Locomotive Association. The association has rebuilt more than six miles of abandoned Southern Pacific track on the north side of Niles Canyon, where the transcontinental railroad track was laid. They plan to extend the track from Vallejo Mills Park in Fremont to a point outside Pleasanton. Rides are open to the public the first and third Sunday of every month during the winter, and every Sunday during the summer and fall. For more information, check its Web site or call (925) 862-9063.

Ride west down Niles Canyon Road with Alameda Creek on your left. After a couple of miles turn right onto Palomares Road, just after the train bridge. Traffic is moderate in Niles Canyon on weekends, heavy on weekdays during commute hours. Palomares Road sees little traffic in secluded Stonybrook Canyon. Sycamore, madrone, dense growths of poison oak, and buckeye line the road.

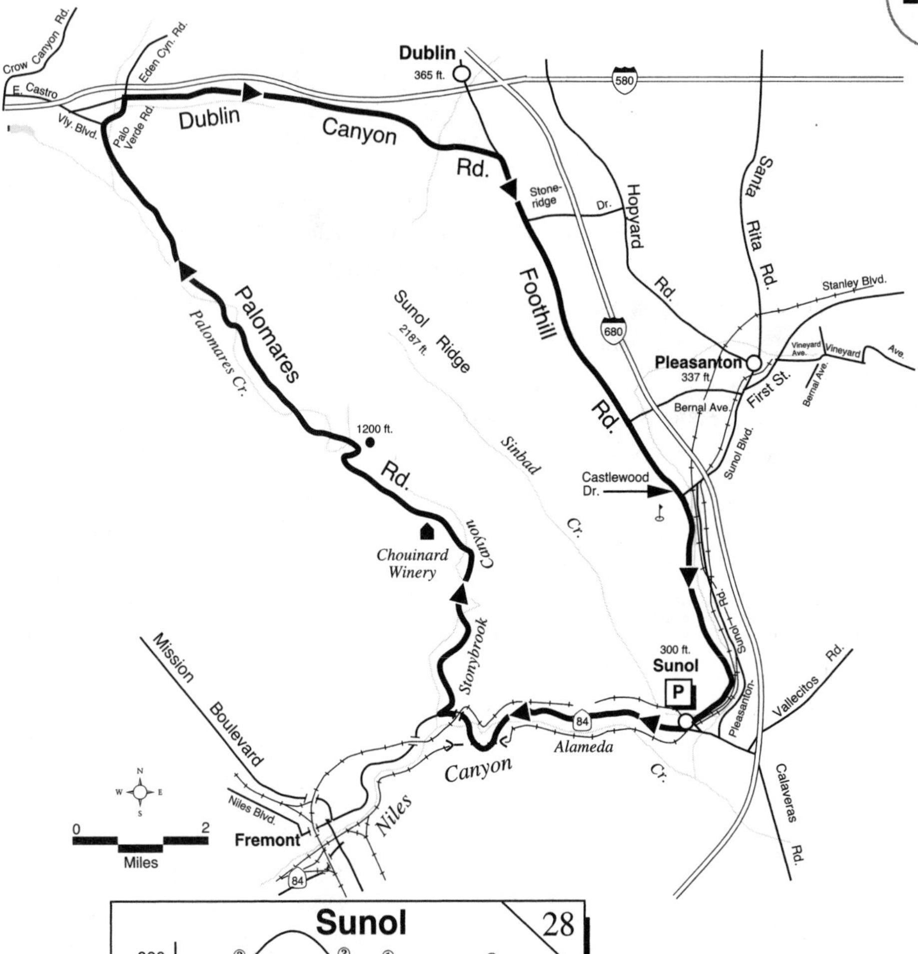

Crow Canyon Rd.

E. Castro

Vly. Blvd.

Palo Verde Rd.

Eden Cyn. Rd.

Dublin
365 ft.

Dublin   Canyon   Rd.

I-580

Stone-ridge

Dr.

Hopyard   Rd.

Santa Rita Rd.

Stanley Blvd.

Palomares

Palomares Cr.

Sunol Ridge
2187 ft.

Foothill

Rd.

I-680

Pleasanton
337 ft.

First St.

Vineyard Ave.

Vineyard Ave.

Bernal Ave.

Sunol Blvd.

1200 ft.

Rd.

Sinbad

Cr.

Canyon

Chouinard Winery

Stonybrook

Castlewood Dr.

Sunol Rd.

Pleasanton Rd.

Vallecitos Rd.

300 ft.
Sunol
P

Mission

Boulevard

Niles Blvd.

Fremont

84

Niles

Canyon

Alameda   Cr.

84

Calaveras Rd.

N
W   E
S

0   2
Miles

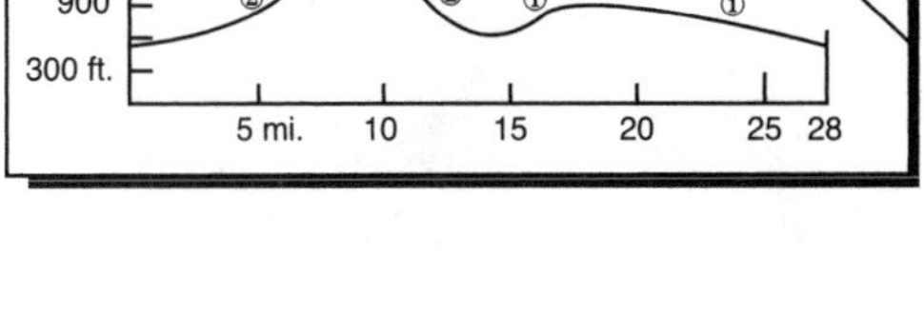

Sunol   28

900

300 ft.

②   ②   ①   ①

5 mi.   10   15   20   25 28

Several miles up the road, you'll pass Westover Vineyard and the Chouinard winery and vineyard. The Chouinard family offers wine tastings on weekends, and some wine is made from the on-site vineyard, which was planted in 1979.

Climb for several miles, and then start a brisk descent into a valley with horse ranches, white picket fences, and cherry orchards. Leave Palomares Road and enter Dublin Canyon on Dublin Canyon Road, which parallels Interstate 580. There's a 2-mile climb followed by a 2-mile descent into Pleasanton.

The ride complexion changes from rural canyons to housing developments and modern office buildings in Amador Valley. Dublin Canyon Road becomes Foothill Road in Pleasanton.

You have two options for riding to Sunol: take Foothill or Pleasanton–Sunol Road, next to Arroyo de la Laguna. On Foothill Road there's a gradual climb on a lightly traveled road, culminating with a panorama of Sunol Valley and Calaveras Canyon to the south.

Castlewood Country Club, at the intersection of Castlewood Drive and Foothill, was built by Phoebe A. Hearst, mother of the publisher William Randolph Hearst. She called this lavish resort Rancho el Valle de San Jose.

MILEAGE LOG

0.0 Start mileage at Sunol General Store. Ride west on Highway 84 (Niles Canyon Road).

4.2 Right on Palomares Road immediately after railroad bridge, beginning climb. 7.5 Westover Vineyard. 7.7 Chouinard vineyard and winery. 8.6 Summit.

13.7 Right on Palo Verde Road at stop sign.

14.1 Right on Dublin Canyon Road at stop sign. 19.2 Name changes to Foothill Road in Pleasanton.

24.0 Left on Castlewood Drive at stop sign if you return on Pleasanton–Sunol Road (otherwise, continue on Foothill Road). Right again onto Pleasanton–Sunol Road after crossing bridge. Right on Niles Canyon Road, cross Arroyo de la Laguna, and then right again on Main Street to return to Sunol.

27.5 End ride in Sunol.

Atherton

29

DISTANCE >>> 13 miles

TERRAIN >>> A few easy hills

TRAFFIC >>> Light to moderate

HOW TO GET THERE >>> Menlo Park can be reached by Caltrain or Highway 101. Take the Willow Road cloverleaf exit, west. Turn right on Middlefield Road at the traffic light. Go less than a half-mile and turn left on Ravenswood Avenue at the traffic light. In less than a half-mile, turn left on Laurel Street at the traffic light. Drive a short distance and turn right onto Mielke Drive, where there's parking at Burgess Park.

IN THE LATE 1800s, ATHERTON, MENLO Park, and other peninsula towns became popular summer retreats for San Francisco's wealthy. Southern Pacific Railroad owners Leland Stanford, Collis Huntington, Charles Crocker, and Mark Hopkins built magnificent estates here. They were joined by mining tycoon Jim Flood, banker William Ralston, and spice baron Arthur Schilling.

Today Atherton's quiet, tree-lined streets retain their historic and rural character. Financiers, businessmen, entertainers, and sports legends live here in relative seclusion.

Start the ride at Menlo Park City Hall, next to Burgess Park. The ride takes you through downtown Menlo Park, past the swank Drager's grocery store, where you might see some luminaries shopping if you stop for a cappuccino at the upstairs café.

Sand Hill Road takes you from an urban to a rural setting. The four-lane divided road has some of the world's most influential venture capital firms. It contracts to two lanes with wide shoulders past Interstate 280. On the way, you'll ride by the entrance to the Stanford Linear Accelerator, where scientists conduct research on subatomic particles.

Sand Hill Road is one of the oldest logging roads in the area, dating back to the days of the Spanish settlers in the early 1800s. Although the Spanish used mostly clay for building material, they needed wood for roofing and framework. Later it became a stage route. True to its name, the road is built on loose sandstone. As late as the 1930s, before the

MILEAGE LOG

0.0 Start mileage at corner of Mielke Drive and Alma Street. Parking available at Burgess Park. Ride northeast on Mielke to Laurel Street.

0.1 Left on Laurel Street at stop sign.

0.2 Left on Ravenswood Avenue at traffic light. Becomes Menlo Avenue.

0.8 Left on University Drive at stop sign.

1.1 Right on Middle Avenue at stop sign.

1.8 Right on Olive Street at stop sign.

1.9 Left on Oakdell Drive in a short distance.

2.5 Left on Santa Cruz Avenue at stop sign.

2.7 Left at traffic light, staying on Santa Cruz Avenue.

3.0 Right on Sand Hill Road at traffic light. Begin 1.1-mile climb. 3.8 Stanford Linear Accelerator entrance. 4.7 Interstate 280 overpass. 4.9 Begin 0.5-mile climb.

6.0 Right on Whiskey Hill Road.

7.3 Right on Woodside Road (Highway 84) at stop sign.

8.5 Right on Northgate Drive immediately after flashing sign "Signal Ahead."

8.9 Left on Stockbridge Avenue.

9.8 Right on Euclid Avenue.

10.0 Left on Polhemus Avenue at T intersection.

10.4 Right on Selby Lane at stop sign.

10.7 Left on Atherton Avenue at stop sign.

10.8 Right on Barry Lane.

11.0 Left on Faxon Road at stop sign.

11.1 Right on Elena Avenue at stop sign.

11.3 Left on Park Lane at stop sign.

11.7 Right on Emilie Avenue at stop sign.

12.0 Left on Valparaiso Avenue at stop sign.

12.6 Right on Laurel Street at stop sign.

13.2 Right on Mielke Drive. End ride.

---

road was paved, cars became stuck in the sand. A scene from the movie *Harold and Maude* was filmed at the top of the hill to the right.

Jasper Ridge Biological Preserve, visible to the southwest from the top of Sand Hill Road, occupies wooded land to the southwest. Every Northern California plant habitat can be found on the 1,200-acre Stanford University nature preserve. The habitat was established in the 1960s, and its recreation facilities were closed to the public in the 1970s.

Turn right on Whiskey Hill Road and climb a short hill. At the stop sign on Woodside Road, turn right and begin the descent to Northgate Drive. Make another right and climb some more on quiet, residential streets. Follow the map carefully through Atherton back to Menlo Park; many of the road signs are short white posts.

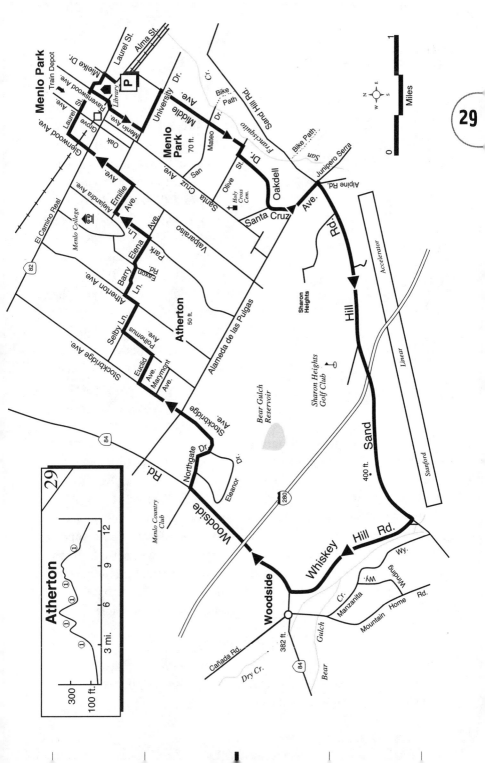

Golden Gate Park

DISTANCE >>> 11 miles

TERRAIN >>> Mostly flat; a few gentle hills

TRAFFIC >>> Light to moderate

HOW TO GET THERE >>> From Interstate 280, take the Highway 1 Pacifica exit. Go about a mile and take a right at the Skyline Boulevard exit. Go for about 3 miles to Lake Merced. Turn left at a stop sign onto the Great Highway. It's a couple of miles to John F. Kennedy Drive and free parking along the ocean. Look for the Dutch windmill at the entrance to Golden Gate Park.

SAN FRANCISCO BICYCLISTS KNOW all about steep streets, traffic congestion, and a shortage of car parking, but follow my route and you'll avoid these hassles while seeing the most beautiful sections of the city. The route includes such popular attractions as the Golden Gate Bridge, the Pacific Ocean, Golden Gate Park, and the Presidio. Do this ride on a Sunday morning when traffic is light. In nice weather the park's roads are lined with parked cars by midday.

The ride starts at the esplanade on the shores of the Pacific. There's plenty of free parking here, but arrive early. You'll start at the Dutch windmill at the intersection of John F. Kennedy Drive and the Great Highway. Be prepared for cool, foggy weather.

Head into Golden Gate Park on John F. Kennedy Drive up a gradual hill. The huge, thickly forested park extends 3 miles inland. John McLaren, a Scottish landscape gardener who was park superintendent from 1887 to 1943, shaped sand dunes and scrub into an urban forest, complete with secluded meadows and picnic tables. Kennedy Drive is closed to cars every Sunday, from 5 A.M. to 5 P.M. On Kennedy you'll pass shallow ponds, grazing buffalo, and the De Young art museum.

Leaving the park, you'll pick up Fifth Avenue, a quiet residential street lined with Victorian-style homes. Watch for traffic at several intersections with only two-way stops. At the end of Fifth Avenue look back to see the rolling hills of San Francisco and Twin Peaks.

A gap in this wall on Fifth Avenue allows entrance to the Presidio.

Soon you'll enter the Presidio, where the ride complexion changes from busy residential to urban forest. You'll pass military housing scattered among the pine trees and cypress. The Presidio is slowly being converted from a military base to Golden Gate National Recreation Area land, as the U.S. government closed the base in 1994. The land has been used for military purposes since Spain occupied it in 1776, followed by Mexico and, from 1848 on, the United States.

A World War II memorial to Americans buried at sea overlooks the Pacific at Kobbe Avenue and Lincoln Boulevard. Turn left on Kobbe and left again on Lincoln for a fast descent along the ocean cliffs. At the bottom of the hill you'll enter the exclusive Pacific Heights neighborhood. Its lavish Mediterranean-style houses have spectacular views (to go with their breathtaking prices), looking out over the Golden Gate Bridge and the Marin headlands.

Farther along, you'll begin climbing at the entrance to Lands End and Lincoln Park golf course on the left. Turn left at the Palace of the Legion of Honor art museum, which was closed due to earthquake damage in 1989 and later retrofitted. This World War I memorial is patterned after the Palace of the Legion of Honor in Paris.

Descend past the golf course to Funston Avenue, where there's a short, gradual climb followed by a short descent to El Camino del Mar. Finally, make a swift descent to the Great Highway past the Cliff House

MILEAGE LOG

30

0.0 Ride east on John F. Kennedy Drive from the Great Highway, past the Dutch windmill.

0.3 Left at stop sign, continuing on John F. Kennedy Drive. 0.8 Buffalo herd on left in field.

1.0 Keep straight at junction. Spreckels Lake on left.

1.9 Keep straight at 4-way stop. Ride under Cross Over Drive (Highway 1). 2.4 Rose garden.

2.7 Left just after stop sign onto Eighth Avenue. De Young Museum on right.

2.9 Right on Fulton Avenue at traffic light.

3.1 Left on Fifth Avenue. 3.6 Geary Boulevard traffic light.

4.1 Ride through gap in stone wall at end of Fifth Avenue after a short, steep climb. Immediate right on West Pacific Avenue, a service road bordering Presidio Golf Course. Ride around barricade and continue through golf course parking lot. 4.3 Continue left on Arguello Boulevard after stop sign, entering Presidio. 4.4 Inspiration Point on right.

6.2 Left on signed Washington Boulevard before Arguello begins descent. 6.5 Military housing. 7.5 Stay on Washington at Harrison Boulevard junction.

7.6 Left on Kobbe Avenue at stop sign.

7.65 Left on Lincoln Boulevard at stop sign and begin fast descent. 8.8 Road name changes to Camino del Mar. 9.0 Lands End entrance and Lincoln Park golf course on left. Great views of the Golden Gate Bridge.

9.5 Left on Legion of Honor Drive. Palace of Fine Arts on right.

9.9 Right on Clement Street at stop sign. Begin gradual climb. 10.6 Street name changes to Seal Rock Drive.

10.1 Left at stop sign onto El Camino del Mar.

10.2 Right on Point Lobos Avenue at traffic light. Begin fast descent past Cliff House restaurant. Watch for cars backing out. Road name changes to Great Highway at bottom of hill.

10.9 End ride.

Restaurant. As you pass the Cliff House, watch for cars backing out from parking spaces. The Cliff House, overlooking Seal Rock, was built in 1858. The house was originally assembled from lumber salvaged off a wrecked schooner. The restaurant has burned down and been rebuilt several times.

If you're interested in riding south along the ocean, there's a recreation path on the east side of the Great Highway, or you can ride along the highway's wide shoulder. The San Francisco Zoo is located on Sloat Boulevard near the Great Highway.

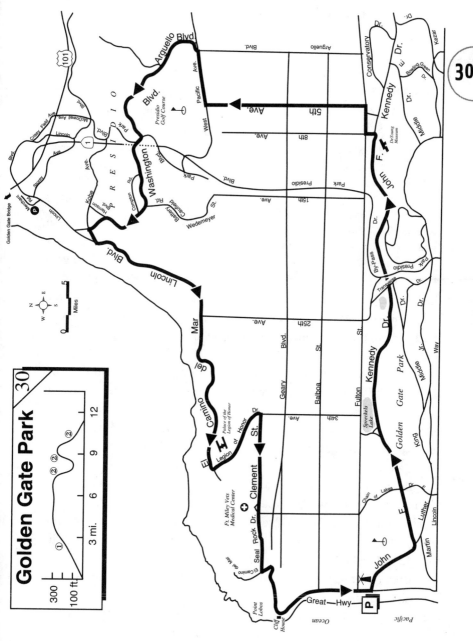

Golden Gate Park

300 ft

100 ft

3 mi.   6   9   12

30

Hillsborough

DISTANCE >>> 13 miles

TERRAIN >>> One long hill

TRAFFIC >>> Light

HOW TO GET THERE >>> From Highway 101, take the Third Avenue exit west. Drive about a half-mile to South B Street and turn left. Parking is available behind Talbot's or along the railroad tracks. Caltrain stops at downtown San Mateo.

HILLSBOROUGH, A STATELY COMMUNITY tucked away in the hills of the San Francisco Peninsula, may never be affordable, but for a modest investment in time and energy you can enjoy this beautiful town by bicycle.

A brief but grand tour of Hillsborough's estates begins in downtown San Mateo. Start near Talbot's, a well-known bicycle store and hobby shop on the corner of South B Street and Fifth Avenue; phone (650) 342-0184. Ride west on Fifth Avenue. In a couple of blocks you'll reach Central Park, where there's a Japanese garden behind a high fence, next to the tennis courts.

Cross El Camino Real and take a right at the next stop sign, on Dartmouth Road; there's a huge bay tree across the street. Dartmouth jogs left in one block. Cross West Third Avenue at a traffic light. Continue straight for a block to Arroyo Court, campsite of the first Gaspar de Portola expedition. The captain and his men stayed here in 1769, a few days after discovering San Francisco Bay.

Return to West Third Avenue and make your way to Crystal Springs Road. The narrow two-lane road winds gently uphill through a canyon carved out by San Mateo Creek. Polhemus Road, the last junction before Skyline, is named for Charles Polhemus, the director of the Southern Pacific Railroad in the 1860s.

During the climb to Skyline Boulevard, you'll ride under four massive concrete pillars supporting Interstate 280's Doran Bridge. Crystal Springs Dam's concrete wall shows itself straight ahead. When completed in 1887, it was the largest concrete dam in the world. The dam withstood the 1906 earthquake undamaged.

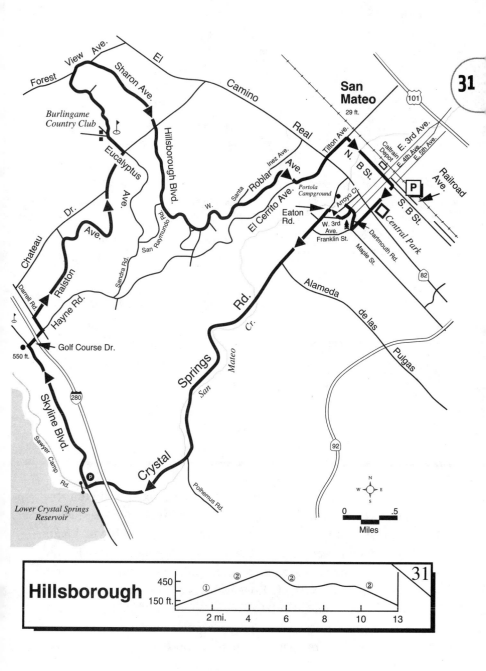

31

Forest View Ave.

El

Sharon Ave.

Burlingame Country Club

Camino

Real

San Mateo
29 ft.

101

Tilton Ave.

E. 3rd Ave.

Caltrain Depot

E. 4th Ave.

E. 5th Ave.

Eucalyptus

Ave.

Hillsborough Blvd.

Santa

Inez Ave.

Roblar

Ave.

El Cerrito Ave.

Portola Campground

N. B St.

Railroad Ave.

P

S. B St.

Chateau

Dr.

Ave.

San Raymundo Rd.

W.

Arroyo Ct.

Eaton Rd.

W. 3rd Ave.

Franklin St.

Dartmouth Rd.

Central Park

Ralston

Sandra Rd.

Maple St.

82

Darrell Rd.

Hayne Rd.

Golf Course Dr.

550 ft.

Springs

Rd.

San

Mateo

Cr.

Alameda

de las

Pulgas

Skyline Blvd.

280

Sawyer Camp Rd.

P

Crystal

Polhemus Rd.

92

Lower Crystal Springs Reservoir

N
W   E
S

0   .5

Miles

Hillsborough

450

150 ft.

① ② ② ②

2 mi.   4   6   8   10   13

31

MILEAGE LOG

0.0 Start mileage at the intersection of East Fifth Avenue and South B Street in downtown San Mateo. Talbot's Bike Shop is located on the corner. Ride west on East Fifth Avenue. 0.1 Japanese garden and tennis courts on left at Laurel Avenue. Follow path through park to see garden behind high wooden fence.

0.4 Right on Dartmouth Road at stop sign. Note giant bay tree.

0.5 Dartmouth jogs left. Cross West Third Avenue at stop light. Location of the Portola expedition along San Mateo Creek. Turn around.

0.7 Right on West Third Avenue at traffic light.

0.8 Right on Eaton Road.

0.9 Left on Crystal Springs Road at stop sign.

1.6 Left at stop sign, staying on Crystal Springs Road.

3.3 Right, staying on Crystal Springs Road at Polhemus Road junction.

4.2 Right on Skyline Boulevard at stop sign.

5.4 Right on Golf Course Drive at stop sign. 5.6 Go straight at stop sign.

5.7 Left on Darrell Road, around circle.

5.9 Right on Ralston Avenue at stop sign.

7.5 Right on Chateau Drive at stop sign.

7.8 Left on Eucalyptus Avenue at stop sign. 7.9 Keep right at junction.

8.6 Right on Forest View Avenue at stop sign.

8.9 Keep right on Sharon Avenue. 9.1 Sharon Avenue becomes Hillsborough Boulevard.

10.4 Left on West Santa Inez Avenue. 10.7 Keep left at junction.

10.9 Bear right onto Roblar Avenue.

11.4 Left onto El Cerrito Avenue at stop sign. Becomes Tilton Avenue.

12.0 Right on North B Street.

12.5 End ride at Fifth Avenue and B Street.

Turn right at Skyline Boulevard, or you can extend the tour by riding straight on Sawyer Camp Trail, behind the gate (see Casual Rides). Climb on Skyline for 1.3 miles, turning right on Hayne Road, and ride under Interstate 280. Descend Ralston Avenue and turn left on Eucalyptus to ride past the exclusive Burlingame Country Club and golf course. President Teddy Roosevelt visited the club while campaigning in 1903. Founded in 1892 (at a different site) by San Francisco socialites, the club attracts the Peninsula's rich and famous. The road through the golf course passes imposing white eucalyptus. Stay on

Eucalyptus until Forest View Avenue, where there's an equally impressive stand of cypress lining the road.

Forest View winds around the golf course and heads south, becoming Sharon Avenue and then Hillsborough Boulevard. Sharon Avenue is named for Senator William Sharon of Nevada, one of the early town builders on the Peninsula. There's a short, steep climb before you begin descending. You'll find some of the oldest and grandest of the Hillsborough estates at the bottom of the hill.

31

Hillsborough was incorporated in 1910. To maintain its privacy, the town annexed 8 square miles, all the way to Crystal Springs Dam, and does not permit business. Another contributor to privacy is the confusing street layout. Pay close attention to the roads, or you might wind up in Half Moon Bay.

Old La Honda Road

DISTANCE >>> 39 miles

TERRAIN >>> Hilly

TRAFFIC >>> Light to moderate

HOW TO GET THERE >>> To reach Woodside, take the Woodside exit from Interstate 280 and go about a mile. From Highway 101, take the Highway 84 exit going west. It's about 5 miles to Woodside. Caltrain stations Redwood City, Menlo Park, and Palo Alto will also work.

OLD LA HONDA ROAD DOESN'T HAVE much traffic on the way from Portola Valley to Skyline Boulevard. This advantage and the fact that it's close to Palo Alto makes it the premier gateway for bicyclists heading to Skyline. It climbs steeply enough to make the ride a pleasantly memorable experience, especially if you're an active rider.

Many bicyclists start their rides in Woodside, a forested community known for its stately mansions and horse ranches. The town dates back to the mid-1800s, when logging was the main industry. Its stores and hotels served wagon masters carrying logs to the port of Redwood City. Today's roads through Woodside carry cars, bicycles, and equestrians on busy weekends.

Cycling is so popular here, bicyclists outnumber cars on most weekends. Ride carefully, and obey all traffic laws.

Old La Honda Road, one of the oldest logging roads in the area, was extended to La Honda in 1876. Like many early roads in the Coast Range, it became a toll road—the Redwood City and Pescadero Turnpike.

Leave Woodside and ride south on Mountain Home Road, where you'll pass palatial estates hidden behind tan oak, eucalyptus, Scotch broom, and redwoods. The road was built in 1872 to link Woodside with the town of Searsville. In the late 1880s, Searsville was abandoned and flooded out with the damming of San Francisquito Creek. Portola Road cuts across the reservoir's marshy backwaters.

Some historical landmarks are located at the beginning of Old La Honda Road. Preston Road, on the right, was formerly Portola Road. Watch for a stairway on your right just after you cross Dennis Martin Creek. It once led to a house owned by spice mogul August Schilling.

Alpine Road leads to redwood country in San Mateo County.

Schilling owned a lavishly landscaped 300-acre estate; the main house was torn down in 1953. The original guest house is on the right, before you cross the creek. Millionaire Edgar Preston built the mansion in the 1870s, along with a pond, hiking trails, flower gardens, and other amenities.

At the first hairpin, crossing Dennis Martin Creek, the driveway straight ahead is the former Dennis Martin Road, the site for some of the earliest logging in the Coast Range. On the right, the trail following a branch of Dennis Martin Creek goes to the Schilling pond, owned by the Midpeninsula Regional Open Space District.

About 2 miles into the climb there's a steep right bend in the road where, in the stagecoach days, passengers had to disembark and walk— or push the wagon—until they reached more level ground. Near the summit, the redwood forest turns even the sunniest days into twilight.

Cross Skyline Boulevard, called "Wonder Way" when it was conceived in 1917. The road, built from 1920 to 1929, extends 47 miles south from San Francisco. Skyline was widened and given its present alignment in the 1950s and 1960s.

MILEAGE LOG

0.0 Start mileage at Woodside School on Highway 84, 0.2 miles west of Cañada Road intersection. Ride east on Highway 84.

0.2 Right on Mountain Home Road at four-way stop. 0.6 Manzanita Way on left.

2.2 Left on Portola Road at stop sign.

2.4 Right at stop sign, staying on Portola Road.

2.8 Right on Old La Honda Road. Begin 3.4-mile climb. 6.2 Skyline Boulevard. Cross road and continue on Old La Honda Road. Begin descent.

8.8 Left on Highway 84 at stop sign. Stop, look, and listen before crossing at blind corner. 12.0 La Honda. Grocery store and restaurant on right in shopping center.

12.7 Left on Pescadero Road.

13.8 Continue straight onto Alpine Road in the redwoods. (Pescadero Road veers right here.) 5.6-mile climb begins in one mile. 17.5 Entrance to honor camp and Pescadero Creek Park on right.

17.9 Left at stop sign. Right goes to Portola State Park. 21.3 Skyline Boulevard. Cross and continue on Page Mill Road. 22.0 Alpine Road junction on left, behind green gate. Dirt road for 2.6 miles connects with paved Alpine Road.

27.1 Keep left at junction with Moody Road. 27.3 Entrance to Foothills Park. Drinking fountain outside gate.

29.6 Left on Arastradero Road.

31.6 Left on Alpine Road at stop sign.

32.8 Right on Portola Road at stop sign.

36.1 Keep straight at junction. Road name changes to Sand Hill Road, unmarked.

36.8 Left on Manzanita Way near bottom of hill.

38.1 Right on Mountain Home Road at stop sign.

38.5 Left on Highway 84 at stop sign.

38.7 End ride at Woodside School.

Begin a descent on Old La Honda Road, which was paved for the first time in 1987. Turn left on Highway 84 at the stop sign, where there's a blind corner. Listen carefully for cars coming up the hill. Hot weekends bring out sun worshipers, who occasionally clog the wide two-lane highway. The descent into the town of La Honda can be marked by a sudden and dramatic drop in temperature entering the redwoods.

Turn left on Pescadero Road after riding through La Honda, and continue straight onto Alpine Road at the bridge over Alpine Creek.

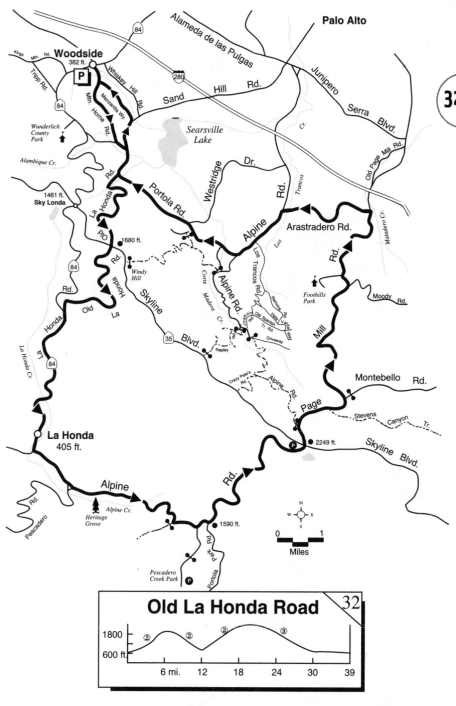

Old La Honda Road

Shortly, you'll pass Heritage Grove, saved from logging in the late 1960s and added to Sam McDonald County Park. The redwoods marked for cutting still have their blue paint.

Alpine Road climbs like a staircase, with steep sections between an 8- and 10-percent grade. You'll have impressive views of the Pacific Coast, the Coast Range, and Mindego Hill to the north.

Cross Skyline Boulevard at the summit, and proceed on Page Mill Road. Parts of Page Mill were built by William Page, a gold miner turned woodsman. Page built the road in 1866 to reach his mill, located in Portola State Park.

Old La Honda Road has some narrow sections wide enough for one car.

At the time it was built, the road was called the Mayfield and Pescadero Road. Mill was interested in the most direct route, and damn the horses. Some grades rise as steeply as 17 percent. Passengers taking the stagecoach to Pescadero must have had a thrilling journey.

Page Mill's steepest section begins midway down, at a hairpin, Shotgun Bend, so called because it used to be a popular shooting area. Turn left on Arastradero Road at the bottom of Page Mill, and return to Woodside through Portola Valley on Alpine, Portola, and Mountain Home roads.

Pescadero Road

DISTANCE >>> 28 miles

TERRAIN >>> Several moderate hills

TRAFFIC >>> Light

HOW TO GET THERE >>> To reach Pescadero from Interstate 280, take the Woodside exit west. It's about 15 miles to Highway 1 on Highway 84. Turn left on Highway 1 and drive about 7 miles south to Pescadero Road, where you'll turn left to arrive at Pescadero in less than 2 miles.

REMOTE CANYONS, PRISTINE STREAMS, and quiet farm towns in the southwest corner of San Mateo County give bicyclists plenty to see and enjoy here. Your ride starts in the coastal town of Pescadero and loops around on Stage Road, Highway 84, and Pescadero Road.

Pescadero looks a lot like it did a century ago. Gordon Moore, Intel's chairman of the board in the 1990s, grew up here and commented it's the only town in the area that's smaller today than it was when he was a boy. Alan Hynding, in his book *From Frontier to Suburb*, compared it to a New England community. Its original four hundred residents lived quiet, pastoral lives. A thriving lumber industry upstream on Pescadero Creek helped maintain the town's four stores, livery stables, and two hotels. Later, dairy farming became the town's mainstay.

Head north on Stage Road, the old coast highway. You'll ride through a long, wide valley, with eucalyptus trees lining the road and horses grazing in meadows. You may hear the cry of a peacock at Willowside Farm, at the end of a row of eucalyptus. In this bucolic setting, an incongruous piece of art stands tall in the farm's front yard. Perhaps watching *The Terminator* inspired the artist to create a 10-foot-tall iron skeleton carrying a 50-caliber machine gun. Who knows?

Begin a short, easy climb where the road circles a hayfield. In the middle of the field there's a metal shed used for testing electronic equipment. The location was chosen for its isolation from radio transmissions. At the summit, you'll have a panorama of Stage Road as it winds down to Pomponio Creek and then up the next ridge. You'll

MILEAGE LOG

0.0 Start mileage at the intersection of Stage Road and Pescadero Road in Pescadero. Ride north on Stage Road. 0.1 North Street on right. 2.4 Begin first 1-mile climb on Stage Road. 4.5 Begin final 0.8-mile climb on Stage Road.

7.1 Right on La Honda Road (Highway 84) at stop sign. Restrooms across the road at San Gregorio General Store.

14.6 Right on Pescadero Road at green sign to Sam McDonald Park.

15.7 Keep right on Pescadero Road at Alpine Road junction. Begin 1.6-mile climb. 16.3 Sam McDonald County Park entrance. Restrooms and water. 17.3 Haskins Hill summit. 19.9 Entrance to Memorial Park. Restrooms and water. 21.3 Loma Mar Store. Portable toilet, water, food. 25.8 Butano Cutoff on left. 26.3 Phipps Ranch on left.

26.5 Right on North Street.

27.4 Left on Stage Road at stop sign.

27.5 End ride in Pescadero.

---

have two descents before reaching San Gregorio. After crossing San Gregorio Creek, you can see the old stagecoach stop on the left at Highway 84. The San Gregorio General Store across the highway stays open seven days a week.

Turn right on La Honda Road (Highway 84) and ride up a wide agricultural valley. Typically you'll have a tailwind, but headwinds farther inland. The road climbs gradually as it follows San Gregorio Creek.

About a quarter-mile from where you'll turn right, look for a log cabin on the right. Ken Kesey, author of *One Flew Over the Cuckoo's Nest* and *Sometimes a Great Notion*, lived here in the 1960s. His wild parties with the late Timothy Leary and other Merry Pranksters attracted national attention, not to mention the county sheriffs.

Turn right onto Pescadero Road at the green road sign for Sam McDonald County Park. You'll pass the park headquarters (water and restrooms here) on the right in a half-mile. Pescadero Road was built by the county in 1876.

From the top of Haskins Hill you can see Butano Ridge to the south. Now begin a long, sweeping descent to Memorial Park and Loma Mar. Don't miss a stop at the Loma Mar store, which has a lounge with

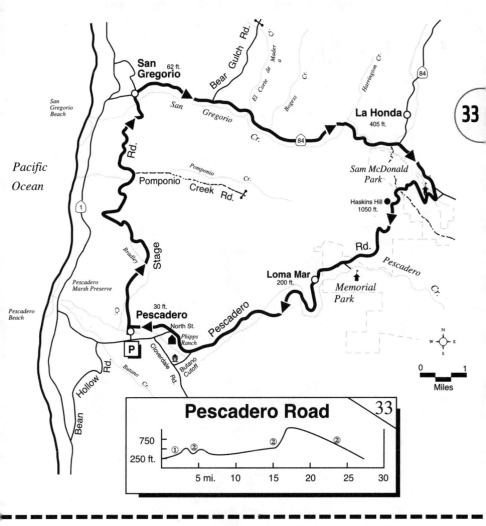

Pescadero Road

33

a television, pool table, fireplace, and tables outside where you can soak up the sun on warm days. From Loma Mar, the road twists and turns as it follows Pescadero Creek through the redwoods. Watch for the pink and red flamingos on your right across the creek. The road leaves the canyon and passes through farmland, with Pescadero High School on the left. It's flat all the way into town.

Portola Valley

DISTANCE >>> 16 miles

TERRAIN >>> Gently rolling hills

TRAFFIC >>> Moderate

HOW TO GET THERE >>> From Highway 101, exit on University Boulevard going west. It's about 2 miles through downtown Palo Alto to the Stanford University campus. University becomes Palm Drive. Turn left on Campus Drive East at the traffic light. From Interstate 280, take the Sand Hill Road exit east. Drive about 2 miles before turning right onto Alpine Road at the traffic light. Immediately enter the left lane and make a left onto Junipero Serra Boulevard at traffic light. Turn left on Campus Drive West. Follow map in book.

"THE LOOP," AS IT'S KNOWN TO local cyclists, draws a parade of fair-weather riders clad in colorful jerseys on Sunday mornings. It's the place to ride and be seen.

Start riding from the Stanford University stadium and continue through the campus to Alpine Road. The Costanoan Indians used the same route centuries ago. Antonio Buelna, the first recorded settler in Portola Valley in 1839, drove a horse and wagon on the road when it was called the Old Spanish Trail. Today, Alpine Road has a wide shoulder and a recreation path on the south side, but it's narrow and bumpy and is popular with walkers and runners. If you ride the path, yield at driveways and intersections.

Alpine Road climbs gradually, passing meadows, oak-covered hills, homes, a country club, and baseball and soccer fields. Coyote, fox, and bobcats occasionally show themselves near the road. Alpine Inn, the oldest roadside tavern in California (founded 1840), is located at the intersection of Arastradero Road.

Turn right onto Portola Road at the stop sign, where there's a convenience store, a gas station, and a small shopping center. Portola Valley's town center is a mile and a half from Portola and Alpine roads. City council meetings are held in a school built over the San Andreas Fault, which formed the valley.

Andrew Hallidie, inventor of the cable car, lived in Portola Valley in the 1880s. He built an experimental tramway from the

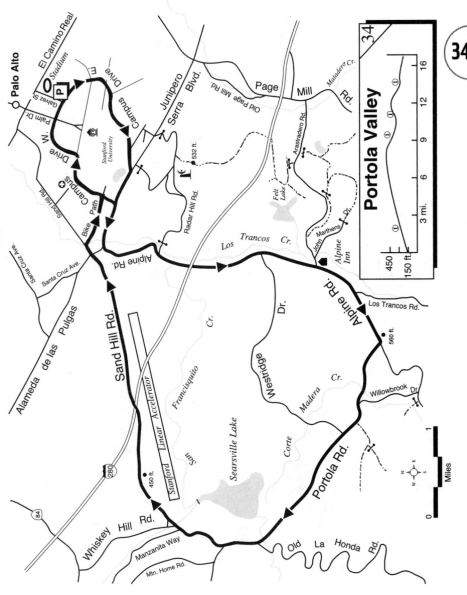

Portola Valley

O Palo Alto

El Camino Real

Galvez St.
Stadium
P
Palm Dr.
W. Campus Drive
Stanford University
Drive
Campus
Campus Path
Bike Path
Sand Hill Rd.

Santa Cruz Ave.

Alameda de las Pulgas

Sand Hill Rd.

280

84

Whiskey Hill Rd.

Manzanita Way
Mtn. Home Rd.

450 ft.

Stanford Linear Accelerator

Searsville Lake

San Francisquito Cr.

Corte Madera Cr.

Westridge Dr.

Los Trancos Cr.

Dr.

Cr.

Alpine Rd.

Junipero Serra Blvd.

Radar Hill Rd.

532 ft.

Old Page Mill Rd.

Page Mill Rd.

Matadero Cr.

Arastradero Rd.

Felt Lake

John Marthens Dr.

Alpine Inn

Los Trancos Rd.

560 ft.

Willowbrook Dr

Portola Rd.

Old La Honda Rd.

Portola Valley

450
150 ft.

3 mi.   6   9   12   16

N
W   E
S

0   1
Miles

MILEAGE LOG

0.0 Start mileage on Stanford University campus next to Stanford Stadium on Galvez Street. There's plenty of parking available next to Angel Field at Eucalyptus Drive. Ride west on Galvez Street.

0.1 Left on Campus Drive East at stop sign.

1.7 Right on Junipero Serra Boulevard at traffic light. 2.1 Campus Drive West intersection.

2.7 Left on Alpine Road at traffic light. 5.7 Arastradero Road intersection. Alpine Inn on left.

6.9 Right on Portola Road at stop sign. 9.7 Old La Honda Road intersection.

10.3 Keep right at junction. Begin Sand Hill Road. Portola Road goes left. 10.9 Manzanita Way intersection. 11.0 Whiskey Hill Road intersection. Begin climb. 11.7 Top of hill. 12.4 Interstate 280. 14.0 Santa Cruz Avenue intersection.

14.2 Right onto multi-use path immediately after crossing San Francisquito Creek bridge.

14.7 Left on Campus Drive West at stop sign.

16.0 Left on Galvez Street. End ride.

34

valley floor into the mountains, across the road from the shopping center.

You'll have a gradual downhill as you leave town. In a curve near the bottom of the hill, you'll pass Old La Honda Road, a popular climb (see page 136). Portola Road crosses a marshy inlet of the Searsville reservoir. In the 1860s, Searsville was located nearby. The town grew on the strength of the logging industry and a short-lived silver "strike." But in 1879, the federal court ordered the town's residents to relocate and make way for the reservoir, which was built in 1891. The drinking water was intended for San Francisco, but it was never used for that purpose. Today the reservoir and the land around it comprise the Stanford Jasper Ridge preserve.

Return on Sand Hill Road, one of the oldest roads in San Mateo County. It was used as early as the 1790s by Spanish settlers harvesting timber for the Bay Area's missions. At the top of the climb on Sand Hill, you'll have a grand view of the bay and the East Bay hills. Descend to Santa Cruz Avenue and continue straight. Cross San Francisquito Creek and immediately turn right on a bike path to reach Campus Drive West. Turn left and return to the stadium.

San Bruno Mountain

35

DISTANCE >>> 14 miles

TERRAIN >>> Two moderate hills

TRAFFIC >>> Light to moderate

HOW TO GET THERE >>> From southbound Highway 101, exit Bayshore/Cow Palace. Drive south on Bayshore to Guadalupe Canyon Parkway, turn right on Guadalupe Canyon Parkway, and drive uphill about 2 miles to the park entrance on the right. From Highway 101 northbound, exit Brisbane/Cow Palace (northbound) or South San Francisco (southbound). Turn north onto Bayshore and drive about 2 miles to the intersection with Guadalupe Canyon Parkway. Turn left and drive uphill about 2 miles to the park entrance on the right. From Interstate 280 southbound, exit Mission Street, then turn left on Market Street, which becomes Guadalupe Canyon Parkway. Continue driving east to the park entrance on the left, about 3 miles from the freeway. From northbound Interstate 280, take the Junipero Serra Boulevard exit. Go left on Junipero Serra, then right on San Pedro Road, which becomes Market Street and then Guadalupe Canyon Parkway.

THE BARREN SLOPES OF SAN BRUNO Mountain rise like a pyramid on the narrow San Francisco Peninsula. Although only a few trees grow on the mountain, the drab exterior reveals fragile beauty when seen up close by bicycle. Thanks to the efforts of conservationists, much of the mountain has been preserved as open space. You can ride to the summit to be rewarded with spectacular views of San Francisco.

On your ride you'll see numerous lush glens, which support the endangered San Bruno Elfin and Callippe Silverspot butterflies, and fourteen species of rare or endangered plants. A prolonged battle between developers and environmentalists ultimately resulted in a 2,326-acre park. The Save San Bruno Mountain citizen's group is devoted to preserving open space. In 1978, San Mateo County and the state purchased 1,500 acres, and more acreage was donated. The mountain has 12 miles of hiking trails and a paved road to the summit, where you'll find TV transmission towers.

The tour starts from the park's main staging area. You'll begin with a brisk descent to the bay and a ride on Old Bayshore Boulevard, where

MILEAGE LOG

0.0 Start mileage at entrance to Mt. San Bruno County and State Park and Guadalupe Canyon Parkway. Left from parking lot onto Guadalupe Canyon Parkway.

2.1 Right on Bayshore Boulevard at traffic light.

4.4 Right on Hillside Boulevard extension.

8.6 Right on Guadalupe Canyon Road at traffic light.

10.5 Right at gate, directly across from entrance to Mt. San Bruno Park entrance. Start climbing Radio Road. 12.0 Summit parking lot. Return same way.

13.5 Keep right and ride through parking lot, followed by Guadalupe Canyon Road underpass.

13.7 End ride at main parking lot.

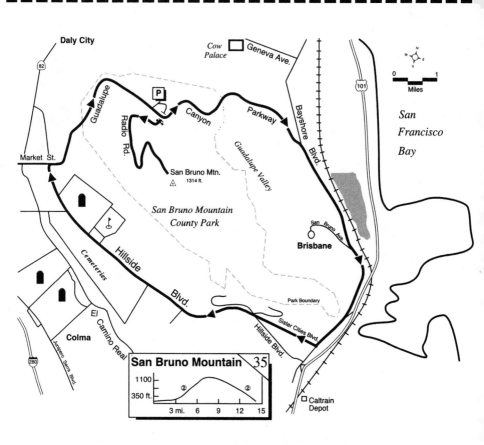

the popular 1968 car-chase thriller *Bullitt* was filmed. The boulevard takes you past the secluded town of Brisbane. Old Bayshore was the main highway along the Peninsula until the mid-1960s, when Highway 101 was opened.

Turn right on the new Hillside Boulevard extension, and ride up a short, steep hill. As you round the western side of the mountain, you'll pass a hodgepodge of industrial parks, cemeteries, and commercial flower gardens in the town of Colma. Near Olivet Memorial Park, on the north side of Hillside, there's even a pet cemetery.

Colma was a thriving agricultural town in the late 1800s. In the 1890s, the character of the land changed dramatically as farm plots were replaced by burial plots. Colma became forever linked with cemeteries in 1907 when San Francisco banned burials within its city limits and turned to the town for burial space. The Catholic Holy Cross Cemetery, founded in 1887, became the first of more than a dozen cemeteries. At least a million people are buried in Colma, including newspaper publisher William Randolph Hearst and lawman Wyatt Earp. The town wasn't incorporated until 1941, with five hundred living residents.

East Market Street, with its many small stores, becomes Guadalupe Canyon Parkway, beginning a gradual 1.8-mile climb to San Bruno Mountain Park. In the past, there has been a New Year's Day San Bruno Mountain race, going from the base of the mountain to the summit.

Your ride finishes dramatically with a 1.4-mile climb to the summit on a road closed to cars. One day as I was riding up, I saw a fox saunter across the road, stop, and watch me as I rode by. At the summit, the Marin headlands and the Golden Gate Bridge fill the northern horizon like a picture postcard.

Admission to the parking area is $4 per car, free for bicycles. The park has picnic tables, restrooms, and a drinking fountain.

It can be cold and windy on the mountain, so dress appropriately. In contrast, during an inversion you may find the weather cold and hazy at the base of the mountain but warm and sunny on top.

Tunitas Creek Road

DURING THE LOGGING BOOM OF THE late 1800s, Tunitas Creek Road and Kings Mountain Road saw wagons carrying redwood logs to Santa Clara Valley. Today the roads serve a small population of mountain residents, as well as cyclists who enjoy riding through the redwoods.

The ride starts in Woodside at the base of the Coast Range. The first mile avoids Woodside Road. In the summer you can help yourself to blackberries growing along Albion Road. You'll need the energy, because Kings Mountain Road has a 10-percent grade right after the Woodside Store museum, and averages 7 percent most of the way.

The store—built in 1854—is Woodside's oldest building. Tripp Road, where the store stands, is named after Woodside Store owner Robert Tripp—dentist, saloon keeper, postmaster, and one of the original San Mateo County supervisors. His business thrived on trade with loggers and teamsters hauling logs to the ports of Redwood City and Alviso.

Kings Mountain Road climbs to Skyline Boulevard through redwoods, oaks, bay laurel, and tan oak. The road signs around these parts have bullet holes, put there by our best marksmen. However, the Huddart Park sign's big, bold yellow letters made from thick steel plate don't have a scratch. Midway up the narrow road there's a wide straightaway. In the mid-1960s, the county replaced a wooden bridge and widened the road. Locals didn't appreciate the widening. Coincidentally, other parts of Kings Mountain Road went without repair for the next fifteen years.

Tunitas Creek Road in San Mateo County passes through a secluded redwood forest on the way to the Pacific Ocean.

Near Skyline Boulevard you'll pass the site of Summit Springs Hotel, where mountain men once met mountain women to play a friendly game of checkers. The building has long since been torn down.

Tunitas Creek Road begins at Skyline and extends to the coast. It was called Froment's Road when built in 1868 by Eugene Froment, who used it for hauling logs from his sawmill at the Lobitos Creek Cutoff junction on Tunitas Creek. It was a toll road until the county bought it in 1884 for $3,000. The road was paved in 1936.

There's a gradual descent for 2 miles, followed by steep hairpin curves; the road often gets wet in the winter and on foggy summer mornings. Some of the old logging roads nearby include Purisima Creek, Swett, Richards, Shingle Mill, Grabtown, and Lobitos Creek. Star Hill, another toll road, went to the coast, but unfortunately San Mateo County abandoned the road after buying it. Purisima Creek

MILEAGE LOG

0.0 Start mileage at Woodside Town Hall and School on Highway 84, 0.2 miles west of the Cañada Road intersection. Ride west on Highway 84, also called Woodside Road.

0.1 Right on Albion Avenue.

0.3 Left on Manuella Avenue.

0.9 Right on Kings Mountain Road at stop sign. 1.3 Woodside Store on left at Tripp Road. 2.8 Huddart Park entrance. 4.1 Road widens briefly.

5.7 Skyline Boulevard junction at stop sign. Cross Skyline, and Kings Mountain Road becomes Tunitas Creek Road. 6.9 Star Hill Road on left. 7.9 Trailhead to Purisima Creek Road on right, beginning steeper descent. 8.7 Shingle Mill Road on left. Private property. 10.4 Mitchell Creek Road on left. Private property. 11.3 Lobitos Creek Road on right.

13.0 Keep left. Lobitos Creek Cutoff on right. Paved road to Highway 1.

15.0 Left on Highway 1 at stop sign. 16.0 Old entrance to Star Hill Road on left.

16.6 Left on Stage Road.

17.7 Left on Highway 84 at stop sign and San Gregorio General Store. 19.8 Bear Gulch Road on left. Goes to Skyline Boulevard, crossing private property. 24.8 Ken Kesey house on right. 25.8 Pioneer Market in La Honda on left. 29.1 Old La Honda Road on right. 31.9 Skyline Boulevard. 35.3 Portola Road on right. 35.7 Wunderlich County Park on left. 36.4 Tripp Road on left.

37.4 End ride at Woodside School.

Road, north of Tunitas Creek, can be reached by taking the Grabtown trail on the right (described in Mileage Log).

At Highway 1 you'll see flower farms. Turn left, cross Tunitas Creek bridge, and begin a half-mile climb. Highway 1 has a wide shoulder most of the way to Stage Road, at the top of the hill.

Turn left on Stage Road and descend to San Gregorio. There's a gradual climb on Highway 84 to Skyline Boulevard and the village of Sky Londa through a wide valley with flower and pumpkin farms. The steepest part of the climb comes a couple of miles above La Honda in the redwoods. From Sky Londa, descend Highway 84 to Woodside through a dense growth of redwoods. Watch out for the first few curves; they can be wet and oily. Continue straight at the bottom of the hill, and it's only a couple of miles into town under the shade of eucalyptus.

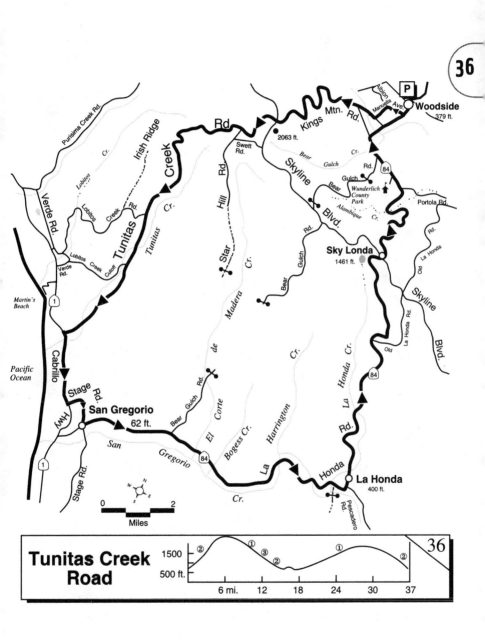

Purisima Creek Rd.
Irish Ridge
Cr.
Lobitos
Lobitos Creek Rd.
Tunitas Creek
Rd.
Kings Mtn. Rd.
2063 ft.
Albion Ave.
Manuella Ave.
P
Woodside
379 ft.
Swett Rd.
Bear
Gulch
Cr.
Skyline
84
Verde Rd.
Tunitas
Cr.
Star Hill Rd.
Bear
Gulch
Wunderlich County Park
Alambique
Cr.
Portola Rd.
Lobitos Creek Cutoff
Verde Rd.
de Madera Cr.
Blvd.
Sky Londa
1461 ft.
Rd.
Rd.
1
Martin's Beach
Bear
Gulch
La Honda Rd.
Old
Skyline
Pacific Ocean
Cabrillo
Hwy
Stage Rd.
Bear Gulch Rd.
El Corte
Bogess Cr.
Harrington
La Honda Cr.
Old
84
Blvd.
San Gregorio
62 ft.
84
La
Honda
Rd.
La Honda
400 ft.
1
San
Gregorio
Stage Rd.
Cr.
Pescadero Rd.
0   2
Miles
N
W   E
S

Tunitas Creek Road

1500
500 ft.

②   ①   ③   ②   ①   ②

6 mi.   12   18   24   30   37

Aptos

DISTANCE >>> 40 miles

TERRAIN >>> Hilly

TRAFFIC >>> Light to moderate

HOW TO GET THERE >>> From Highway 17, take the Summit Road exit and go south about 3 miles to Summit School. Parking is available on the left just beyond the pedestrian overpass.

ON THIS RIDE TO APTOS YOU'LL HAVE a chance to see apple orchards in secluded coastal valleys sheltered by redwoods, ideal country for bicycling. Your ride starts by following the crest of the Santa Cruz Mountains separating Santa Clara Valley from the Pacific Ocean. Buildings along the road, including Summit School where the ride begins and ends, received extensive damage from the 1989 Loma Prieta earthquake, whose epicenter was nearby.

Summit Road has a fair amount of traffic on weekends because it's the main artery for mountain residents traveling to Highway 17. You're only on it for a mile, though, before a 5-mile descent on San Jose–Soquel Road. The two-lane road's gentle curves and smooth surface make for a fast descent. Then the road leaves the mountains and flattens out on the coastal plain, an ideal growing location for greenhouses along the wooded Soquel Creek.

The town of Soquel dates back to the 1700s, when it was settled by the Spanish. One of the oldest buildings in Aptos, the Bayview Hotel, dates back to the turn of the last century; you can find it at the intersection of Trout Creek Road and Soquel Drive. Soquel grew rapidly when logging started in the late 1800s. Once the easily accessible trees had been cut, Aptos residents turned to planting fruit trees. Some large orchards still do business today, but they face an uncertain future as Aptos grows.

After a stretch on busy, four-lane Soquel Drive, the ride returns to a rural experience, heading inland on Trout Gulch Road. You'll wind your way through quiet redwood canyons with tree-lined creeks. Valencia Road becomes a wonderland of pink and white apple blossoms

The earth shifted a foot or more on some sections of Summit Road east of Highway 17 during the 1989 Loma Prieta earthquake.

in the spring. Passing apple orchards and then entering redwood forests affords a unique experience of nature's diverse beauty.

At the junction of Valencia and Bear Valley Roads you'll see two white buildings, a post office and a meeting hall, built by German-born Frederick Hihn in the 1880s. Hihn made his fortune logging the nearby redwoods. The buildings are now historic landmarks.

There is a short, steep climb and a descent before you reach Corralitos, a farming town with a grocery market known for its smoked meats. After eating one of the store's excellent sandwiches, you can power your way up Eureka Canyon. The secluded canyon road follows Corralitos Creek through the redwoods.

On a hot summer day you'll appreciate the frequent shady sections under a canopy of redwoods and, higher up, tan oak. There's a mile-long descent; then you'll have more climbing on Highland Way, which rises like a staircase and passes numerous places where massive landslides closed the road in years past. After a final, fast descent the ride finishes on Summit Road.

MILEAGE LOG

0.0 Start the ride just beyond the pedestrian overpass on Summit Road, at the yellow school crossing sign. 0.5 Burrell School, classic one-room school (now a winery), on right. 0.7 Summit Store on left.

0.9 Right on San Jose–Soquel Road at T junction. 1.5 Begin descent, until 7.0. 8.8 Casalegno Store on right.

12.0 Left on Soquel Drive at traffic light. Begin bike lane following Pacific Coast Bike Route. 12.2 Begin 0.3-mile climb. 14.0 Cabrillo College. 15.2 Shopping center on right with grocery stores, delicatessens, and other stores.

15.5 Cross under train subway and keep left at Y junction, riding over bridge. 15.6 Aptos Creek Road.

15.7 Left on Trout Gulch Road at stop sign.

16.2 Right on Valencia Road at Y junction. 17.3 Apple orchards.

18.3 Keep right at junction with Valencia School Road.

18.7 Left onto Day Valley Road; begin 0.4-mile climb.

20.6 Left on Freedom Boulevard at stop sign after steep descent.

20.7 Left on Hames Road; begin 0.2-mile climb followed by 0.2-mile descent.

21.3 Right on Pleasant Valley Road at stop sign.

21.4 Left on Hames Road; begin climb. 21.9 Begin descent.

Highland Way experiences frequent landslides, like this one in 1998. County road crews needed a year to make repairs.

22.9 Left on Eureka Canyon Road at stop sign. Corralitos Market and Sausage Company on right. No facilities until Summit Store in 16 miles. 31.1 Road pavement is all patches here.

31.7 Summit and four-way junction. Road name changes to Highland Way. 33.6 Popular parking area for mountain bike riders entering the Soquel Demonstration Forest. 33.9 Begin stair-step climb. 34.6 Devastated hill from previous landslide.

37.6 Right and immediate left at stop sign onto Summit Road at junction with Spanish Ranch Road and Mt. Bache Road. 38.5 Begin steep one-mile descent.

40.2 End ride at Summit School.

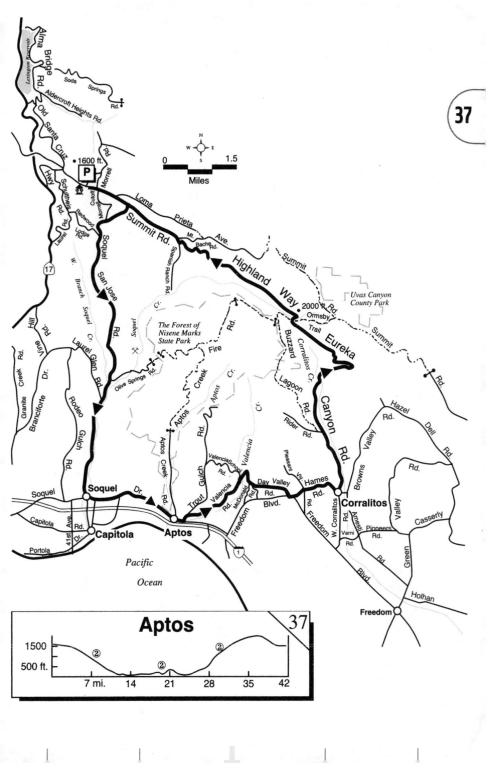

Lexington Reservoir

Alma Bridge Rd.

Soda Springs

Aldercroft Heights Rd.

Old Santa Cruz Hwy

• 1600 ft.
P

Schulthels Rd.

Redwood Lodge Rd.

Laurel Rd.

Morrell Rd.

Morrell Cutoff

Soquel

Loma Prieta Ave.

Summit Rd.

San Jose Rd.

Spanish Ranch Rd.

Mt. Bache Rd.

Summit

Highland Way

2000 ft.

Ormsby Trail

Eureka

Summit

Uvas Canyon County Park

Rd.

W. Branch Soquel Cr.

Vine Hill Rd.

Granite Creek Rd.

Branciforte Dr.

Rodeo Gulch Rd.

Laurel Glen Rd.

Olive Springs Rd.

Soquel Cr.

The Forest of Nisene Marks State Park

Fire

Creek

Aptos Cr.

Aptos

Cr.

Buzzard Lagoon Rd.

Corralitos Cr.

Canyon Rd.

Aptos Creek

Aptos Rd.

Trout Gulch Rd.

Valencia School Rd.

Valencia

Valencia Rd.

McDonald Rd.

Rider Rd.

Pleasant Vly.

Day Valley Rd.

Hames Rd.

Pajaro

Freedom Blvd.

W. Corralitos Rd.

Corralitos

Browns Valley Rd.

Hazel Dell Rd.

Rd.

Valley Rd.

Casserly Rd.

Varni Rd.

Amesti Rd.

Pioneers Rd.

Green Valley Rd.

Freedom

Holhan

Soquel

Soquel Dr.

Capitola Rd.

41st Ave.

Capitola

Portola Dr.

Aptos

Pacific

Ocean

① (1)

Aptos
37

1500

500 ft.

② ② ②

7 mi.   14   21   28   35   42

Big Basin Redwoods Park

38

DISTANCE >>> 57 miles

TERRAIN >>> Hilly

TRAFFIC >>> Light to moderate

HOW TO GET THERE >>> From Highway 17 out of San Jose, take the Saratoga–Los Gatos Road exit, the last exit to Los Gatos. Go north 3.5 miles to downtown Saratoga. Take a left at the traffic light onto Highway 9. From Highway 85, take the Saratoga Avenue exit and stay on it for 2 miles to downtown Saratoga. There's parking off Fourth Street in the center of town, on the right, down a steep hill.

HERE'S A ROUTE FOR CYCLISTS WHO want to see the "big picture"—big redwoods, Big Basin Redwoods State Park, big climbs, and big descents. Start the ride in downtown Saratoga, beginning a 7-mile climb to Saratoga Gap at Skyline Boulevard.

The climb has a steady grade of about 6 percent. Much of the way you'll be climbing in the shade of trees, but from a few places higher up you'll see Stevens Canyon.

Highway 9 follows Saratoga Creek for several miles. Right before crossing the creek, you'll pass Congress Springs campground. This site attracted tourists in 1866, when someone decided to promote the creek's mineral springs as having curative powers. People from all over the world flocked here to drink and bathe. The town of Saratoga had been settled only ten years earlier.

Farther up Highway 9, on the left, there's a driveway to Savannah Chanelle Vineyards, one of many small vineyards in the Santa Cruz Mountains. The winery, established in the 1890s by French immigrant Pierre Pourroy, has a main building dating to 1923.

In the parking lot at Saratoga Gap summit you won't find any facilities, but a food vendor often serves thirsty and hungry riders.

The Skyline to the Sea Trail starts near the southwest corner of the Skyline and Highway 9 intersection and follows the old Saratoga Toll Road for several miles before crossing Highway 9 and continuing to Big Basin Redwoods State Park. Bicycles are prohibited on the toll road.

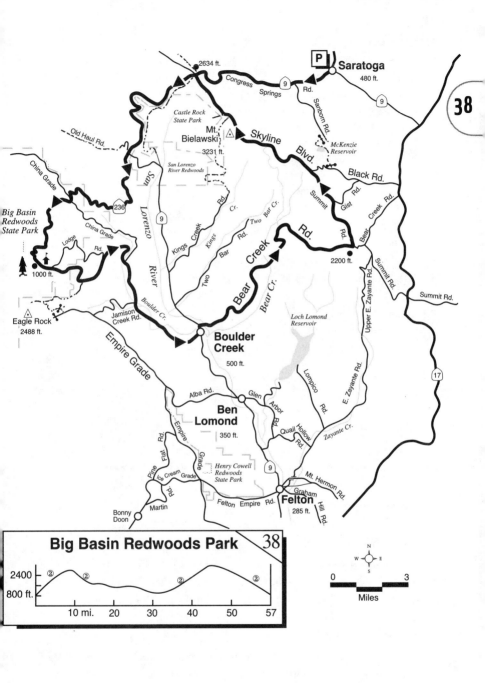

P **Saratoga**
480 ft.

2634 ft.

Congress Springs Rd. ⑨

Sanborn Rd.

⑨

38

Castle Rock State Park

Mt.
Bielawski ⚠ Skyline

3231 ft.

McKenzie Reservoir

Blvd.

Old Haul Rd.

Black Rd.

China Grade

San Lorenzo River Redwoods

San Lorenzo River

⑨ 236

Summit

Gist Rd.

Bear Creek Rd.

Big Basin Redwoods State Park

China Grade

Lodge Rd.

🌲
1000 ft.

China Grade

Cr.

Kings Creek

Kings

Two Bar Cr.

Bear Creek Rd.

Rd.

2200 ft.

Summit Rd.

Summit Rd.

⚠
Eagle Rock
2488 ft.

Jamison Creek Rd.

Bar Rd.

Two Bar

Bear Creek

Bear Cr.

Loch Lomond Reservoir

Upper E. Zayante Rd.

⑰

Boulder Cr.

Boulder Creek
500 ft.

Empire Grade

Alba Rd.

Glen

Arbor Rd.

Quail Hollow Rd.

Lompico Rd.

E. Zayante Rd.

Zayante Cr.

Summit Rd.

Ben Lomond
350 ft.

Pine Flat Rd.

Ice Cream Grade

Empire Grade

Henry Cowell Redwoods State Park

⑨

Mt. Hermon Rd.

Bonny Doon

Martin

Rd.

Felton Empire Rd.

Graham Hill Rd.

Felton
285 ft.

Big Basin Redwoods Park 38

| 2400 | ② | ② | | ② | ② |
| 800 ft. | | | | | |

10 mi.   20   30   40   50   57

N
W ◆ E
S

0   3

Miles

MILEAGE LOG

38

0.0 Start mileage at intersection of Fourth Street and Highway 9 (Big Basin Way) in downtown Saratoga. Parking available at Wildwood Park on Fourth Street. Ride west on Highway 9. 0.5 Hakone Japanese Gardens on left. Road is steep into park. 1.5 Pierce Road junction on right. 3.0 Savannah Chanelle Vineyards on left. 3.3 Dog City. 3.9 Redwood Gulch Road junction on right.

7.0 Skyline Boulevard junction at stop sign. Continue straight on Highway 9.

13.1 Right onto Highway 236 at Y junction. 16.2 Summit.

17.8 Keep straight on Highway 236 at China Grade junction. 18.9 Service Road on right at gate. 21.3 Big Basin Redwoods State Park headquarters on left, with restrooms and water. Food and drink 50 yards on right at store. 24.5 Summit. 28.0 Jamison Creek Road junction on right. Steep road.

30.6 Left at stop sign onto Highway 9 in Boulder Creek. Grocery store and gas station with food and drink located at the corner.

30.7 Right on Bear Creek Road immediately after crossing Boulder Creek Bridge. 35.1 Begin 4.7-mile climb. 39.5 David Bruce and Bear Creek wineries. 39.8 Summit.

40.1 Left on Summit Road. 43.9 Black Road junction on right. Road widens and becomes Skyline Boulevard. 47.2 Summit at 3,000 feet. 47.7 Castle Rock State Park entrance. Restrooms and drinking fountain in parking area.

50.3 Right on Highway 9.

57.3 End ride in Saratoga.

Cross Skyline Boulevard and begin a 6-mile descent to the Highway 236 junction at Waterman Gap. Highway 236, a lightly traveled, narrow, twisty road, climbs gradually through a canopy of tan oak, manzanita, and bay laurel. It was built in the early 1900s to make Big Basin Redwoods State Park more accessible to cars. At the China Grade junction, you can't miss seeing Eagle Rock looming over the thickly forested Big Basin.

Begin descending to park headquarters, where you'll be greeted by impressive stands of ancient redwoods. The park was founded in 1902 to protect the largest remaining concentration of old-growth redwoods in the Santa Cruz Mountains. About 3,500 of the park's 18,000 acres have redwoods dating back to the Crusades. A huge tree ring next to park headquarters puts the trees' life spans into historical perspective. From headquarters you can also see the largest trees in the park. Across the street from Highway 236 there's a store where you can stock up on food and drink.

Continue south on Highway 236, climb out of the basin, and then descend 5 miles to Boulder Creek, a former logging town with plenty of rustic charm. Turn left onto Highway 9, cross Boulder Creek, and immediately turn right on Bear Creek Road. Built in 1875 as a toll road, Bear Creek Road was bought by Santa Cruz County in 1890 for $500.

Now begin a gradual climb for several miles as the road follows Bear Creek. The road eventually takes on a decidedly steeper grade of about 8 to 9 percent for a couple of miles.

Turn left onto Summit Road at the junction and begin a stair-step climb to Black Road. Along the way you'll have views of the San Lorenzo River basin and Los Gatos. The narrow Summit Road becomes the much wider Skyline Boulevard at Black Road. The climb grows more gradual until peaking out at Mt. Bielawski, altitude 3,000 feet. Shortly after the summit, you'll pass the entrance to Castle Rock State Park, a popular hiking and climbing destination. It's all downhill the last 9 miles into Saratoga.

Hicks Road

DISTANCE >>> 26 miles

TERRAIN >>> One steep hill

TRAFFIC >>> Light to heavy

HOW TO GET THERE >>> From Highway 17, take the Saratoga–Los Gatos exit going east. Drive uphill and turn right on Los Gatos Boulevard at a T intersection and traffic light. Go about 1 mile. Street name changes to Main Street. There's parking available along Main Street or on University Avenue.

SAN JOSE EXTENDS SOUTH THROUGH Coyote Valley like the tentacles of an octopus, but it hasn't encroached upon the historic mining camp of New Almaden. The camp still provides a pleasant ride in the countryside.

New Almaden's mercury mines more than helped California's gold rush pan out. Mercury is essential for smelting gold ore. Antonio Suñol of San Jose discovered cinnabar, a red rock yielding mercury when smelted, in the hills above New Almaden. Suñol made his find after the local Indians told him stories about the distinctive red rock. A Mexican cavalry officer confirmed the location in 1845. Alexander Forbes opened the first mine in 1851.

Today the land surrounding the mines makes up the Almaden Quicksilver County Park. The park's mercury mines are mostly located along Los Capitancillos Ridge. Mexican, Chinese, and Cornish miners drilled 2,000-foot-long shafts into the hills, descending well below sea level.

Mining operations finally ended in 1976, and today New Almaden is a quiet rural enclave. In 1974, Santa Clara County purchased 3,598 acres of the mining area for a park. In the late 1990s, park headquarters and the museum were moved to La Casa Grande, a three-story brick building. It's open Friday noon to 4 P.M., Saturday and Sunday 10 A.M. to 4 P.M. The park has miles of trails for hiking and horseback riding, and some were opened to bicycling in 1999 (see Almaden Quicksilver Park mountain bike ride).

As you ride up Hicks Road, imagine what life must have been like for the early-day miners. They might have considered hiking the

MILEAGE LOG

0.0 Start mileage on East Main Street in downtown Los Gatos at the Highway 17 overpass next to Los Gatos Creek Trail. Ride east on East Main. Becomes Los Gatos Boulevard.

0.9 Right on Kennedy Road at traffic light. 1.5 South Kennedy on right; keep left. 3.3 Summit.

4.2 Right on Shannon Road at stop sign.

4.9 Left on Hicks Road at stop sign.

5.9 Right on Camden Avenue at traffic light. 6.6 Summit of short climb from Guadalupe Creek.

8.3 Right on Almaden Expressway at traffic light.

10.0 Right on Almaden Road at traffic light. 12.4 Loma Almaden, museum on left. 12.9 Road name changes to Alamitos Road at Alamitos Creek.

14.5 Right on Hicks Road. 15.0 Begin steep 1.2-mile climb. 16.2 Summit and Mt. Umunhum Road (also called Loma Almaden Road) on left. Begin steep, hazardous descent.

21.4 Left on Shannon Road, beginning climb. 22.6 Summit, followed by swift 1-mile descent.

24.0 Keep left, continuing on Shannon Road at stop sign.

24.8 Left on Los Gatos Boulevard at traffic light. Becomes East Main Street.

26.1 End ride at Los Gatos Creek Trail trailhead and Highway 17 overpass.

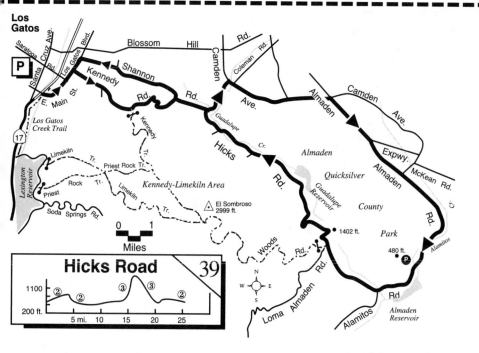

difficult 15-percent grade on "Horrible" Hicks Road a fun way to spend a Sunday afternoon, compared to the hard labor of mining.

Hicks Road was built by Santa Clara County in 1868, at the behest of Thomas Hicks. Hicks and his wife, Josepha Burnell, came into possession of 160 acres of land near what is now Hicks Road. They asked the county to build a road for local landowners. Hicks worked hard to have the road built, gaining support among Mexican locals for his petition. The road was improved in 1878, and again in 1895.

Use caution riding down the northern slope of Hicks Road, which has even steeper sections than the southern slope. After a fast drop from Guadalupe Reservoir, the road descends gently along the tree-lined Guadalupe Creek. The ride up Shannon Road will seem easy after Hicks.

39

Morgan Hill

DISTANCE >>> 22 miles

TERRAIN >>> A few hills

TRAFFIC >>> Light

HOW TO GET THERE >>> From Highway 101, take the Dunne Avenue exit west. Turn right on Depot Street in just less than 1 mile, where there's parking available next to the Caltrain station.

THE TOWN OF MORGAN HILL, 10 MILES south of San Jose, gives a bike rider plenty of opportunity to have some fun on quiet country roads. Maybe that's one reason the well-known Specialized Bicycles calls this community home.

You'll start at the Caltrain depot on Depot Street, a block away from downtown Morgan Hill and busy Monterey Road. Turn onto Dunne Avenue and begin a gradual climb toward 1,800-foot El Toro Mountain. The peak is not "Morgan Hill." The town was named after Hiram Morgan Hill, a rancher who lived here in the 1880s.

You'll pass numerous estates on your way to the aptly named Paradise Valley. Narrow, winding Oak Glen Avenue follows oak-covered Paradise Creek, passing stately country homes surrounded by walnut groves. In the early spring, fields of yellow mustard plants add to the beauty of rolling, oak-covered hills.

Turn right onto Sycamore Avenue and begin a short, steep climb. As you grunt your way up the hill, watch for a farmhouse on the left with clucking hens and the occasional hog lazing in the sun on the property's front yard. Blasting down the hill, you'll pass the homes of numerous Silicon Valley refugees who built houses in this rural paradise.

The pace of life quickens on Watsonville Road, where there's a fair amount of traffic moving at high speed. In less than a mile, though, you'll turn right onto the much less traveled Uvas Road. As you pass over Uvas Creek, note that the peaceful-looking stream occasionally turns into a river, flooding houses and trailer parks that occupy its flood zone.

Uvas Road rolls gently through oak-covered hills, passing the 286-acre Uvas Reservoir County Park on the way. You may see a coyote

MILEAGE LOG

0.0 Start mileage at the corner of Third Street and Depot Street next to the Caltrain station. Ride south on Depot.

0.2 Right on Dunne Avenue at stop sign.

1.0 Left on De Witt Avenue at stop sign.

2.2 Right on Edmundson at stop sign.

2.9 Left on Oak Glen Avenue at stop sign. 3.2 Oak Glen Farms on right.

3.8 Right on Sycamore Avenue at stop sign. 4.3 Begin 0.3-mile climb, followed by descent.

5.9 Right on Watsonville Road at stop sign.

6.5 Right on Uvas Road at junction. 8.8 Restroom on right at parking lot. 12.4 Croy Road entrance to Uvas Canyon County Park.

14.0 Right on Oak Glen Avenue at junction. Immediately after turn keep left at next junction. 15.7 Willow Springs Road on left. 16.6 Chesbro Reservoir parking lot with restroom.

17.1 Right at stop sign.

17.2 Left at junction after crossing creek.

18.7 Left on Edmundson Avenue.

19.5 Left on De Witt Avenue at stop sign.

20.6 Right on Dunn Avenue at stop sign.

21.3 Left on Monterey Road at signal light.

21.4 Right on Fifth Street.

21.5 Left on Depot Avenue at stop sign.

21.7 End ride.

40

---

amble across the road, or a bobcat. Turkey vultures and red-tailed hawks frequent the area, along with the occasional golden eagle.

On Oak Glen Avenue you'll follow the shores of the 269-acre Chesbro Reservoir County Park. The reservoir attracts cormorants, great blue herons, and a variety of ducks. If you're interested in another moderate climb, you can take Willow Springs Road. The last few miles on Oak Glen Avenue bring you back through peaceful Paradise Valley before retracing your route to Morgan Hill.

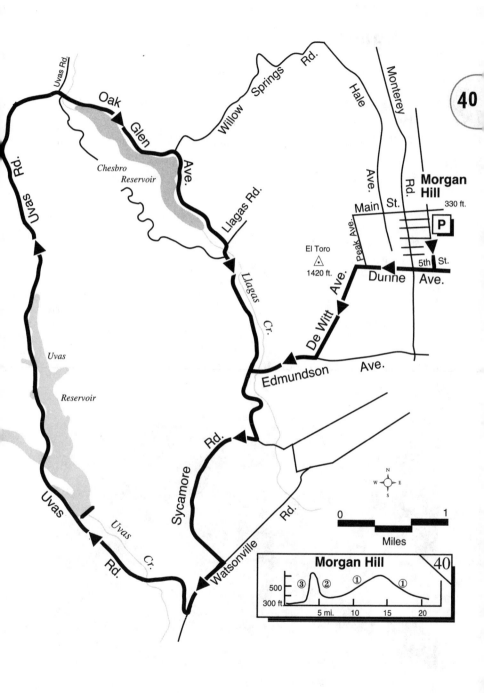

Uvas Rd.

Oak

Glen

Ave.

Willow Springs Rd.

Hale

Monterey

40

Ave.

Rd.

Morgan Hill

330 ft.

Chesbro Reservoir

Llagas Rd.

Main St.

P

Llagas Cr.

El Toro △ 1420 ft.

Peak Ave.

5th St.

Uvas Rd.

De Witt Ave.

Dunne Ave.

Uvas

Reservoir

Edmundson Ave.

Sycamore Rd.

Rd.

N
W ✦ E
S

0   1

Miles

Uvas Rd.

Uvas Cr.

Watsonville Rd.

Morgan Hill

40

500

300 ft.

③ ②   ①   ①

5 mi.   10   15   20

Mt. Hamilton

DISTANCE >>> 102 miles

TERRAIN >>> Hilly

TRAFFIC >>> Light to moderate

HOW TO GET THERE >>> From Interstate 880, take the Calaveras Boulevard exit going east. Drive about 2 miles, going under Interstate 680 and passing the next traffic light at North Victoria Drive. Then take the next right at a dead-end street behind a grocery store. From Interstate 680, take the Calaveras Boulevard exit going east.

ALTHOUGH IT'S THE HIGHEST AND longest climb in the Bay Area, Mt. Hamilton Road is a long way from being the most difficult. In the spring—the best time for riding here—you'll be gasping for breath at the spectacular sight of wildflowers on a canvas of rolling green hills.

This ride doesn't just climb to the summit, an experience in itself. It descends the eastern slope and then loops through Livermore and Sunol. The wild, undeveloped eastern side of Mt. Hamilton has almost no public facilities, surprising considering its proximity to San Jose.

Switchbacks on Mt. Hamilton Road make the climb relatively easy.

Mt. Hamilton Road was built in 1876 to accommodate horses hauling heavy equipment, which is why the climb has a steady 5- to 7-percent grade, interrupted by two descents. On weekends there's a fair amount of traffic in the early going, but it thins out after several miles. The first of two short descents on the climb brings you to Joseph D. Grant County Park, where there's a restroom, drinking fountains, and an old ranch house doubling as a museum and park headquarters.

The road climbs past the park entrance, where, from the edge of the road, you'll have an eagle's view of Halls Valley. In the spring, white wildflowers, looking like freshly fallen snow, carpet the valley floor. Watch for hawks, kites, turkey vultures, bluebirds, kingbirds, woodpeckers, horned larks, and golden eagles soaring over the valley.

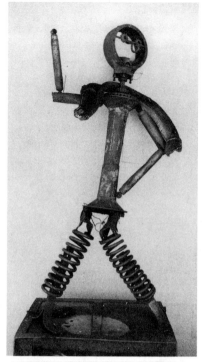

"Car Man" at San Antonio Junction stands guard at the store's entrance.

Following the second descent, to Smith Creek, you'll pass giant manzanita, a bush identified by its polished, dark cinnamon-colored limbs. The last 6 miles has many hairpin turns and the best views of Santa Clara Valley, north to San Francisco and south to the Monterey peninsula.

Lick Observatory's five white telescope domes can be seen for miles around in Santa Clara Valley. The main observatory was constructed in 1887 by James Lick, a real estate magnate. A 36-inch refractor inside the main observatory was one of the largest telescopes of its day. Turn right to reach the main observatory, open to the public on weekends, 1 P.M. to 5 P.M. The post office lobby at the north end of the observatory has drinking fountains and restrooms, open during observatory hours.

MILEAGE LOG

0.0 Start mileage in Milpitas on Calaveras Boulevard at Calaveras Court, one block east of North Victoria Drive. Ride east on Calaveras Boulevard, which becomes Calaveras Road.

0.6 Right on Piedmont Road. In a short distance, on your left you'll see the historic adobe house, behind a new housing development.

4.3 Left on Penitencia Creek Road at traffic light.

4.8 Right on Toyon Avenue.

5.7 Left on McKee Road at stop sign.

6.2 Left on Alum Rock Avenue at stop sign.

6.5 Right on Mount Hamilton Road. 8.4 Crothers Road junction on left. Descends to Alum Rock Park. 12.4 Begin 1.8-mile descent. 14.0 Quimby Road on right. Goes to San Jose. 14.2 Joseph D. Grant County Park on right. Restrooms, drinking fountain, history museum. 17.4 Begin 0.9-mile descent to Smith Creek. Restroom on left. 19.8 Kincaid Road on left. 20.7 Giant manzanita on left.

24.6 Summit. Water available from faucet outside house on right. Observatory uphill to right. Public display open most days. View point. 25.5 Begin descent. 27.6 Emergency water from spring on right. 29.8 End descent at Isabel Creek. Begin 0.6-mile climb followed by 1-mile descent. 33.1 Begin 0.3-mile climb. 34.0 Daffodils and Red Pokers on right. 36.2 Begin 0.8-mile climb followed by 0.7-mile descent. 38.0 San Antonio Valley flower display. 42.7 San Anton Junction bar. Road name changes to Mines Road. 43.7 Begin 2-mile climb. 45.7 Summit. 46.7 Begin 1.1-mile climb. 50.9 Alameda County Line. 62.5 Begin 3.5-mile descent.

66.9 Right at stop sign, staying on Mines Road.

70.4 Left on Tesla Road at stop sign, which becomes Vineyard Road in 0.1 miles.

72.0 Left on College Avenue across the street from City Hall and police station.

73.1 Left on South Fourth Street.

73.2 Right at traffic light on Holmes Street (Highway 84).

73.3 Left on South S Street at break in yellow divider, about 20 yards after road divider ends.

73.4 Left on First Street at stop sign.

73.5 Left on Stanley Boulevard at traffic light. Begin bike lane/wide shoulder.

76.5 Watch out for train tracks crossing Stanley Boulevard.

78.3 Keep straight on First Street at traffic signal. Stay on First Street through Pleasanton. Road becomes Sunol Boulevard. 80.5 Pass under Interstate 680.

80.6 Keep left on Pleasanton Sunol Road.

84.1 Left at four-way stop sign on Paloma Way. 84.8 Ride under Interstate 680. 84.9 Continue straight at stop sign on Calaveras Road. 85.2 Cork oak on right. 88.7 Cross Alameda Creek and begin climb. 91.7 Summit followed by half-mile descent. 98.5 summit.

98.8 Right on Calaveras Road at stop sign. 99.7 Ed Levin County Park on right. Restrooms and drinking fountains.

102 Left on Calaveras Court. End ride.

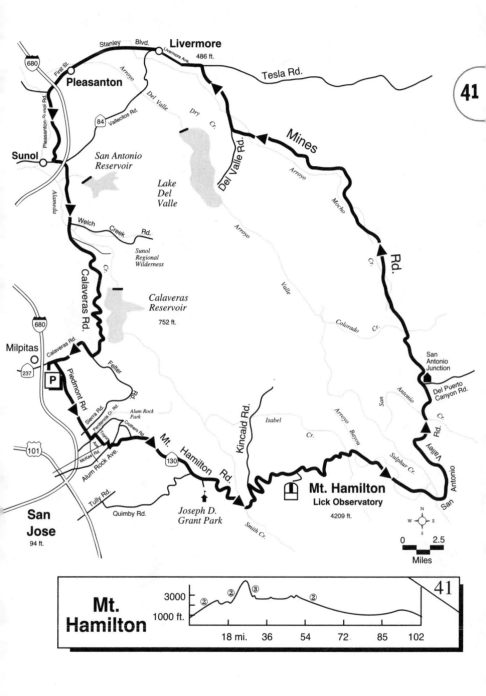

680
Stanley   Blvd.   **Livermore**
486 ft.
First St.   Tesla Rd.
Pleasanton
Pleasanton–Sunol Rd.
84   Vallecitos Rd.   **Mines**
Arroyo
Del Valle
Dry   Cr.   Arroyo
Sunol
San Antonio   Del Valle Rd.   Mocho
Reservoir
Alameda   Lake
Del   Cr.   **Rd.**
Welch   Creek   Rd.   Valle
Arroyo
Sunol
Regional
Wilderness
Calaveras Rd.   Cr.   Valle
Calaveras
Reservoir
752 ft.   Colorado   Cr.
680
Milpitas   San
Calaveras Rd.   Antonio
237   P   Piedmont Rd.   Felter   Rd.   Junction
San   Del Puerto
Sierra Rd.   Antonio   Canyon Rd.
Penitencia Cr. Rd.   Alum Rock
Park   Kincaid Rd.   Cr.   Rd.
101   McKee Rd.   Crothers Rd.   Isabel   Arroyo   Bayou   Valley Rd.   San Antonio
Alum Rock Ave.   Mt.   Hamilton   Rd.   Cr.
130   **Mt. Hamilton**
Tully Rd.   Sulphur Cr.   **Lick Observatory**
Quimby Rd.   Joseph D.   4209 ft.
San   Grant Park
Jose   Smith Cr.   N
94 ft.   W   E
S
0   2.5
Miles

**Mt.
Hamilton**
3000   ② ③
②   ②
1000 ft.
18 mi.   36   54   72   85   102

41

Check your brakes before descending the steep, winding eastern slope, where speeds can exceed 40 mph. Cross Isabel Creek at the bottom, climb a short hill, and descend again to Arroyo Bayou Creek. The old road below followed the creekbed and had numerous fords, but was moved to its present alignment to avoid flooding.

The best wildflower viewing comes at San Antonio Valley, after several more short climbs. A few miles farther along, you'll come to San Antonio Junction, a likely lunch stop considering it's the only store until Livermore. The bar sells everything from hamburgers to soup, soda, beer, and candy bars.

Continue to Livermore on Mines Road, which follows Arroyo Mocho Creek in a narrow canyon. There's a 2-mile and then a 1-mile climb before you come to a long, fast descent to Livermore Valley's vineyards.

Ride through Livermore and pick up the flat, straight Stanley Boulevard into Pleasanton. Stanley has a bike lane and wide shoulders.

Finally, there's the climb up traffic-free Calaveras Road to a ridge at 1,000 feet. Now is a good time to enjoy the blue waters of Calaveras Reservoir and contemplate the five-course meal you'll have after the ride.

Santa Cruz

DISTANCE >>> 51 miles

TERRAIN >>> Hilly

TRAFFIC >>> Light to moderate

HOW TO GET THERE >>> From Highway 17, take the Saratoga–Los Gatos exit going east. Drive up a hill and turn right on Los Gatos Boulevard at a T intersection and traffic light. Go about half a mile. Street name changes to Main Street. There's parking available along Main Street or on University Avenue.

YOU CAN RIDE TO SANTA CRUZ FROM the South Bay via several different routes, but this one has the most scenic, least traveled, and easiest-to-negotiate roads. There's a 1.6-mile stretch of dirt road with a short, steep climb that's rideable on a road bike. The climb up Lexington Reservoir has been paved and is not as steep as it used to be, when it went straight up the face of the dam. Be sure to bring your sense of adventure for this ride.

The ride starts in downtown Los Gatos, where Los Gatos Creek Trail joins East Main Street at the Highway 17 overpass. The wide, mostly flat trail follows Los Gatos Creek through Los Gatos Canyon. You'll see many hikers and cyclists on this well-known trail. If you go right at the bottom of the first short hill that starts the ride, you can see Forbes Flour Mill museum in about 200 yards, the first business in Los Gatos in 1850.

The trail follows the route of South Pacific Coast Railroad, which went through the canyon from late 1880 until 1940, when it was disbanded. The railroad continued into Aldercroft Canyon and then through eight tunnels bored into the Santa Cruz Mountains. If only the tunnels were still open for bicycling! Today you can take a train ride from Felton's Roaring Camp to Santa Cruz, following the original route.

Go left across the dam summit and begin a roller-coaster ride on Alma Bridge Road, which winds around the reservoir. A long climb begins when you cross Los Gatos Creek. Alma Bridge Road merges here with Aldercroft Heights Road. Author Jack London spent summers at a cabin on what is now Santa Cruz Water Company land, near the second tunnel entrance at Morrell Road and Los Gatos Creek.

MILEAGE LOG

0.0 Start mileage on Los Gatos Creek Trail, located at the junction of East Main Street and the Highway 17 overpass in downtown Los Gatos. Walk bike through barrier and ride downhill on dirt trail. Parking available at Lexington Dam if you don't want to ride on the trail. 1.3 Short, steep climb. 1.5 Climb face of Lexington Dam on trail. Stay left of spillway.

1.6 Left on Alma Bridge Road after going through barrier. 4.5 Soda Springs Road.

5.9 Keep right at Aldercroft Heights Road junction. Becomes Aldercroft Heights Road.

6.5 Left on Old Santa Cruz Highway at yield sign. 7.8 Holy City site. 9.1 Mountain Charlie Road on right.

10.1 Left on Summit Road at stop sign.

11.5 Right on Morrell Cutoff. 12.4 creek.

13.3 Right on Soquel San Jose Road at stop sign.

19.8 Right on Laurel Glen Road at Casalegno Store. 22.1 Summit. Becomes Mountain View Road.

23.0 Left on Branciforte Drive at stop sign. 25.9 Granite Creek Road.

27.6 Right on Glen Canyon Road. (If going to Santa Cruz, continue straight on Branciforte. 28.3 Left on Goss Avenue at stop sign. 28.4 Right on Branciforte at stop sign. 29.0 Left on Water Street at traffic light. 29.2 Right on Seabright Avenue at traffic light. 29.3 Left on Soquel Avenue at traffic light, then right back onto Seabright.

30.2 Sullivan's Bike Shop on right just beyond Murray Street. To get to the Boardwalk, take Murray Street toward Santa Cruz for 0.3 miles. Pick up sidewalk starting on East Cliff Drive on left, down to railroad bridge and pedestrian walkway.)

30.6 Keep straight at stop sign. Becomes Green Hills Road.

31.9 Ride through barrier. Becomes Navarra Drive.

32.6 Left on Granite Creek Road at stop sign.

32.7 Left on Highway 17 overpass to Scotts Valley Road.

32.9 Right on Scotts Valley Road at traffic light. Then immediate shallow left at traffic light onto Glenwood Drive. 34.8 Bean Creek Road.

35.7 Left on Mountain Charlie Road. The climb has three steep pitches of about 15 percent, 200 yards each. 39.9 Road levels. 40.4 Spring on left.

40.9 Straight onto Summit Road at stop sign.

41.1 Cross Highway 17 overpass on Summit Road overpass. Left at stop sign and then immediate left onto Mountain Charlie Road.

41.9 Left on Old Santa Cruz Highway at stop sign.

44.5 Right on Aldercroft Heights Road.

45.1 Left onto Alma Bridge Road after crossing Los Gatos Creek.

49.3 Walk down Los Gatos Trail on Lexington Dam.

51.1 End ride at East Main Street.

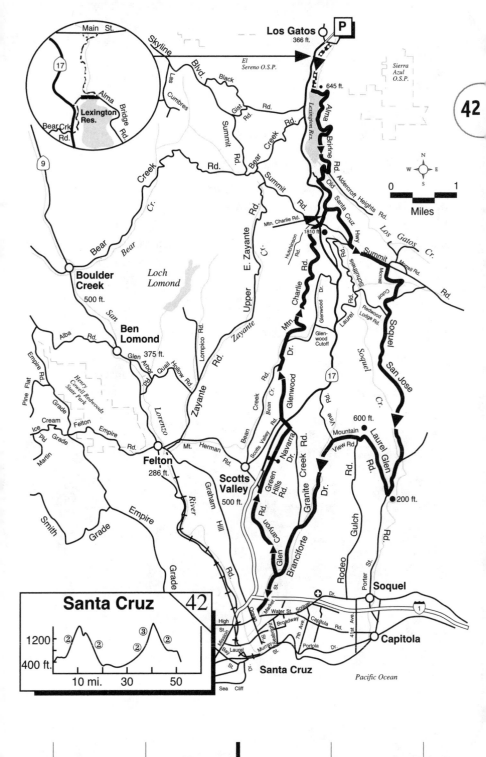

Main St.

Skyline

17

Alma

Bridge Rd.

Bear Crk. Rd.

Lexington Res.

Los Gatos
366 ft.

P

El Sereno O.S.P.

Black

Glen Rd.

Rd.

Blvd.

Las Cumbres

645 ft.

Sierra Azul O.S.P.

42

Lexington Res.

Alma

Bridge Rd.

Aldercroft Heights Rd.

Los Gatos Cr.

9

Summit Rd.

Bear Creek Rd.

Summit Rd.

Old Santa Cruz Hwy

N
W E
S

0   1
Miles

Creek

Cr.

Bear

Bear

Mtn. Charlie Rd.

1810 ft.

Hutchinson Rd.

Summit

Morell Rd.

E. Zayante

Cr.

Upper

Boulder Creek
500 ft.

Loch Lomond

Charlie

Mtn.

Dr.

Glenwood Dr.

Laurel Rd.

Schulteis Rd.

Redwood Lodge Rd.

Morrell Rd.

Summit

Cutoff

Soquel

San Jose

Rd.

Alba Rd.

Ben Lomond
375 ft.

Glen

Lompico Rd.

Quail Hollow Rd.

Arbor Rd.

Zayante

Rd.

Creek

Bean

Cr.

Glenwood

17

Glenwood Cutoff

Laurel

Soquel

Cr.

600 ft.

Empire Flat Rd.

Pine Flat

Grade

Cream

Ice

Rd.

Felton

Empire

Grade

Lorenzo

Felton
286 ft.

Mt. Herman Rd.

Bean Creek Rd.

Scotts Valley Rd.

Navarra Dr.

Mountain View Rd.

Vine Rd.

Laurel Glen

Rd.

Martin

San

Zayante

Graham Hill

Glenwood

Dr.

Green Hills Rd.

Granite Creek Rd.

Rd.

200 ft.

Smith

Grade

Empire

Grade

Scotts Valley
500 ft.

Canyon Rd.

Glen

Branciforte

Dr.

Rodeo Gulch Rd.

River

Grade

Rd.

High St.

Market St.

Water St.

Soquel

Dr.

Broadway

Capitola Rd.

Porter St.

Soquel

Mission St.

Bay St.

Laurel St.

Murray St.

Seabright

7th Ave.

Capitola

Portola Dr.

41st Ave.

1

Capitola

Santa Cruz
42

1200
400 ft.

②   ②   ③   ②
②

10 mi.   30   50

Santa Cruz

Sea Cliff

Pacific Ocean

Fortunately, the long climb on Old Santa Cruz Highway rises at a grade of only about 4 to 6 percent, and traffic is usually light. Although many houses line the road, dense redwood groves keep most of them hidden. Halfway to the summit you'll pass a long building in a clearing on the left, the former site of Holy City, a quirky little community that flourished in the 1930s. The opening of Highway 17 in 1940 reduced traffic on Old Santa Cruz Highway to a trickle, hastening the town's demise.

Old Santa Cruz Highway was, until the early 1940s, the main road to Santa Cruz. Highway 17 began to take its present alignment and size during the 1930s. Before the highways were built, travelers coming from Santa Clara Valley took the Santa Cruz Gap Turnpike toll road, built in 1858, to present-day Summit Road and then to either Old San Jose Road (following today's Soquel San Jose Road) or the Mountain Charlie toll road.

Turn left at the summit on Summit Road and ride to Morrell Cutoff. Some sections of Summit Road were displaced as much as a foot and a half during the Loma Prieta earthquake in 1989. Turn right on Morrell, and begin a steep, bumpy descent to Laurel Creek. The secluded road climbs gradually back to Soquel San Jose Road. (If you want to stop at the Summit Store, continue straight on Summit Road a short distance.)

A paved multi-use path across the face of Lexington Reservoir climbs steeply.

On Mountain Charlie Road don't miss the house made from a giant steel tube.

Begin a long, gradual descent on tree-lined Soquel San Jose Road to Laurel Glen Road. Look for the Casalegno Store at the intersection, which dates back to 1929.

There's a moderate climb on Laurel Glen Road, followed by a gradual descent to Branciforte Drive. At Branciforte and Glen Canyon Road, you can either ride into Santa Cruz on Branciforte according to route directions or ride home by Glen Canyon Road. Glen Canyon climbs gradually to Highway 17, where you'll take Green Hills Road, which becomes Navarra Drive, and then bridge over Highway 17 to Scotts Valley Road.

Turn right and then left at the traffic lights on Scotts Valley Road to begin a gradual climb on Glenwood Highway. Spacious fields give way to redwoods as you climb the bumpy concrete road, which was built around 1914. Turn left on Mountain Charlie Road, where you'll have a chance to test your legs on occasional short, steep stretches. Charles Henry "Mountain Charlie" McKiernan built the road in the 1858 and charged a toll. It must have been a daring adventure to take a wagon down the road, because some sections have grades as steep as 17 percent. But the road climbs like a staircase, with level sections where you can stop and rest. Don't miss the blue silo on your left; a creative designer turned it into a house. At the top of the climb, you'll see Mountain Charlie's homesite on the right. Near here in 1854 the early settler got into a fight with a grizzly bear, narrowly escaping with his life. The road levels here and takes you to Summit Road, crossing Highway 17 by overpass. Take Mountain Charlie Road down to Old Santa Cruz Highway, and retrace your route to downtown Los Gatos.

Stevens Creek Reservoir

DISTANCE >>> 11 miles

TERRAIN >>> One moderate hill

TRAFFIC >>> Moderate

HOW TO GET THERE >>> From Interstate 280 southbound, take the North Foothill Boulevard exit going south. Stay on Foothill for about 3 miles to reach the Stevens Creek County Park headquarters on the left, down a steep hill. From northbound 280, take the Foothill Boulevard exit (a bad intersection with merging traffic). At the end of the ramp take a left at the traffic light and continue south to the park. From Interstate 85, take the Stevens Creek Boulevard exit west. Go about 2 miles and turn left on Stevens Creek Road at a traffic light. It's about 2 miles to the park entrance on the left. Parking costs $2.

RIDING AROUND STEVENS CREEK Reservoir after work has become a popular pastime for cyclists in Silicon Valley. Scenic hillsides, invigorating climbs, and a park setting offer a welcome change from the crowded valley. Start the ride at Lower Stevens Creek County Park on Stevens Canyon Road. If you're interested in mountain bike riding, you can ride up the power-line road and over to Fremont Older Open Space Preserve. From the ridgeline you'll have spectacular views of Santa Clara Valley. The power-line trail starts across the road from park headquarters. It follows Stevens Creek for 0.3 miles before rising steeply.

For the road ride, turn left onto Stevens Canyon Road from the parking lot at park headquarters. Stevens Canyon Road rolls along for several miles, with mostly easy climbs. It follows Stevens Creek through a narrow canyon, where flooding damaged the road in the winter of 1982–83. Begin a moderate climb at Mt. Eden Road, which snakes up to a ridge overlooking a former orchard, now populated by mansions. The historic Garrod Horse Ranch, on the left at the summit, permits bicycles to ride through to reach trails in Fremont Older. Bikes must yield to equestrians and must be walked through the ranch.

A steep descent is followed by a flat section and then a brisk downhill on Pierce Road through the trees to Comer Drive. Just before

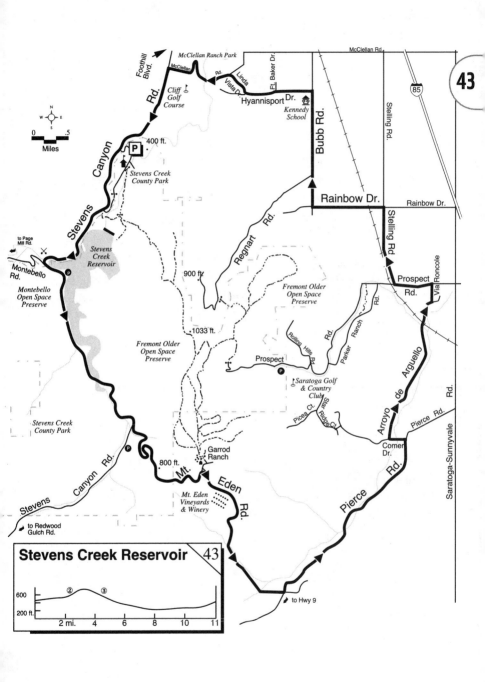

43

McClellan Ranch Park
Foothill Blvd.
McClellan Rd.
Rd.
Linda Vista Dr.
Ft. Baker Dr.
McClellan Rd.
85
Cliff Golf Course
Hyannisport Dr.
Kennedy School
Canyon
Rd.
Bubb Rd.
Stelling Rd.
N
W   E
S
0   .5
Miles
400 ft.
P
Stevens Creek County Park
Rainbow Dr.
Rainbow Dr.
Stevens
Regnart Rd.
Stelling Rd.
to Page Mill Rd.
Stevens Creek Reservoir
Montebello Rd.
900 ft.
Fremont Older Open Space Preserve
Prospect
Rd.
Via Roncole
Montebello Open Space Preserve
1033 ft.
Fremont Older Open Space Preserve
Rolling Hills Rd.
Rd.
Parker Ranch Rd.
Arroyo de Arguello
Prospect
P
Stevens Creek County Park
Saratoga Golf & Country Club
Picea Ct.
Star Ridge Ct.
Pierce Rd.
Saratoga-Sunnyvale Rd.
Stevens Canyon Rd.
P
800 ft.
Mt. Eden Rd.
Garrod Ranch
Comer Dr.
Pierce Rd.
Stevens
Mt. Eden Vineyards & Winery
to Redwood Gulch Rd.
to Hwy 9

Stevens Creek Reservoir 43

600
200 ft.
②   ③
2 mi.   4   6   8   10   11

MILEAGE LOG

0.0 Start mileage at parking lot next to park headquarters for Lower Stevens Creek County Park. Restrooms, drinking fountain. Left at stop sign onto Stevens Canyon Road. 0.6 Stevens Creek Dam parking lot. 1.0 Montebello Road on right. Climbs to Black Mountain and connects with Page Mill.

2.4 Keep left onto Mt. Eden Road at stop sign. Stevens Canyon Road goes right. (Pavement on Stevens Canyon Road ends in 3.7 miles. It's a gentle climb through a beautiful tree-lined canyon.) Begin 0.8-mile climb. 3.2 Top of hill. 3.9 Check brakes. Steep downhill.

4.7 Left on Pierce Road at stop sign.

6.1 Left on Comer Drive. Watch for row of pine trees.

6.2 Right on Arrollo de Arguello.

7.2 Left on Via Roncole at stop sign.

7.3 Left on Prospect Road at stop sign.

7.6 Keep right on Stelling Road. Prospect Road goes to Fremont Older Open Space Preserve and popular mountain bike trail to Lower Stevens Creek Park.

8.1 Left on Rainbow Drive at traffic light.

8.6 Right on Bubb Road at stop sign.

9.3 Left on Hyannisport at stop sign.

9.6 Keep left on Hyannisport.

9.8 Right on Linda Vista Drive.

10.0 Left on McClellan Road at stop sign.

10.6 Left on Stevens Canyon Road at stop sign.

11.3 Left into Lower Stevens Creek County Park parking lot. End ride.

---

turning left onto Comer, you'll pass the remnants of Kennedy Vineyards, one of the last valley vineyards in an urban setting. Turn right onto Arroyo de Arguello and return to where you started on residential streets.

Note that if you ride on Stevens Canyon Road on weekdays, there's heavy truck traffic in and out of the Permanente rock quarry directly opposite the reservoir.

Coyote Hills Regional Park

DISTANCE >>> Up to 21 miles

TERRAIN >>> Flat

TRAFFIC >>> Bicyclists, hikers

HOW TO GET THERE >>> From Interstate 880, take Highway 84 west, exit at Paseo Padre Parkway, and drive north about 1.5 miles. Turn left on Patterson Ranch Road. From Highway 101, take Highway 84 east. Exit on Paseo Padre Parkway and go north. Turn left on Patterson Ranch Road. Parking costs $4 when the kiosk is attended.

COYOTE HILLS REGIONAL PARK offers one of the most unusual geographical settings in the Bay Area. A knoll in the park overlooks the bay and lush reed marshes to the east. There's a history museum, miles of bike paths, picnic benches, and abundant wildlife to view.

You'll understand why the Ohlone people settled here when you visit. Shell mounds left by the Native Americans are evidence of the fruitful bounty they found in nearby Alameda Creek and the bay. Reeds from the marsh were used to make boats, baskets, and huts; the hills have stone suitable for crafting hand tools. You can learn about the Ohlone culture and see their artifacts on display at park headquarters.

A gently rolling path winds around the base of the hills in the 1,021-acre park next to Dumbarton Bridge. For a longer ride, take the path along Alameda Creek; Alameda Creek Regional Trail passes under all road and train bridges. The Army Corps of Engineers built the path as part of a flood control project in 1973. Stay on the south side of the creek in both directions; the north side is designated for horseback riding. You'll see white-plumed egret, great blue heron, and a variety of ducks feeding along the creek.

For an interesting side trip, visit Ardenwood Historic Farm. To get there from the trail, take Ardenwood Boulevard, the first bridge, going south. It's about a mile to the park entrance. The farm depicts life in the 1880s. Farmers use horse and plow to till the land, they milk cows by hand, and the farmhouse has period furniture. You can tour on foot or

MILEAGE LOG

0.0 Start mileage at the visitor center in Coyote Hills Regional Park. Ride southeast on Patterson Ranch Road.

0.3 Right at parking lot and path, where you'll see restrooms and a picnic area. Stay on paved path at all times for this loop.

44

1.0 Right at junction. Apay Way on left. It's 1.6 miles from here to Highway 84 and the National Wildlife Center.

2.6 Keep right to return to visitor center.

3.4 End loop at visitor center.

Ride from visitor center to Niles Canyon on Alameda Creek Regional Trail

0.0 Start at visitor center and ride toward bay on Bayview Trail.

0.8 Right at junction to reach Alameda Creek Regional Trail, followed by immediate right onto Alameda Creek path. 2.5 Union City Boulevard. 3.2 Train tracks. 3.9 Alvarado Boulevard. 4.1 Interstate 880. 5.8 Decoto Road. 6.6 Isherwood Way. 9.3 BART and train tracks. 10.3 Mission Boulevard. 10.5 Old Canyon Road Bridge. End of trail at Niles Canyon. Return by same route.

21.0 End ride.

---

go by horse-drawn flat car on railroad tracks. The park is open Tuesday through Sunday year-round.

Six miles from Coyote Hills, ride under Interstate 880 and then turn south. The path passes rock quarries and railroad yards. In the nearby Niles District during World War I, Charlie Chaplin made five of his early movies with Gloria Swanson.

Apay Way, a dirt road in the park, connects with the National Wildlife Refuge south of Dumbarton Bridge. Dense brush and dill growing along the road provide an ideal habitat for deer and bobcats. Cross Highway 84 on a pedestrian bridge over the toll booths. Cyclists coming from Palo Alto can take a recreation path over Dumbarton Bridge and continue east on a frontage road.

Docents offer guided tours of the refuge by bike and on foot. The East Bay Regional Park District manages Coyote Hills Regional Park and Alameda Creek Regional Trail.

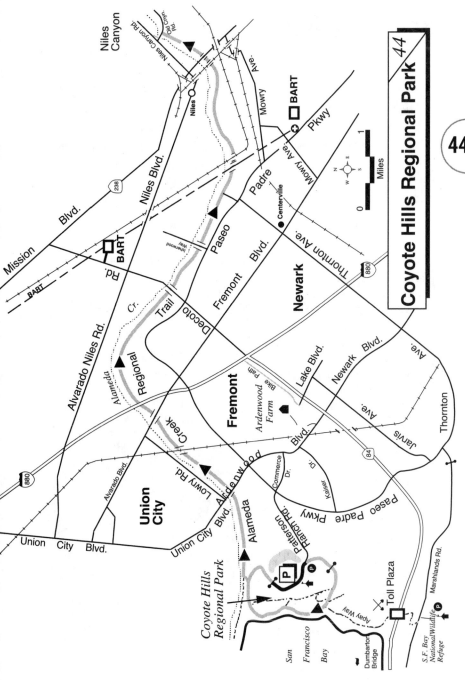

Coyote Hills Regional Park

44

Iron Horse Trail

45

DISTANCE >>> 17 miles

TERRAIN >>> Flat

TRAFFIC >>> Bicyclists, pedestrians, in-line skaters

HOW TO GET THERE >>> From Interstate 680, take the Main Street/Treat Boulevard exit. Southbound traffic needs to turn left from Main Street onto Treat Boulevard. Go about a quarter-mile before turning right onto Oak Road. It's just over a quarter-mile to Walden Park on the left. Parking is limited to about 25 spaces. By BART, get off at the Pleasant Hill Station and ride south on Oak Road, or exit from the rear of the station and take Jones Road south, cross Treat Boulevard, and pick up the trail. A multi-use bridge is planned over Treat Boulevard.

WHEN COMPLETED, THE IRON HORSE Regional Trail will extend more than 40 miles—from Livermore to Suisun Bay—making it the longest multi-use recreation trail in the Bay Area. Riding 80 miles out and back, even on a flat multi-use trail, qualifies as something more than a "casual" ride. Sections of the trail can be seen next to Interstate 680, south of Interstate 580.

This shorter ride explores some of the most scenic and interesting parts of the trail and includes a stop for a tour of the Danville Railroad Museum before turning

around. This route, like most of the Iron Horse Trail, follows a Southern Pacific Railroad right-of-way abandoned in 1977. The flat trail, administered by the East Bay Regional Park District, connects busy downtowns, schools, shopping centers, quiet residential areas, business centers, and parks.

You'll need to cross a busy street only once; the rest of the

Danville's railroad museum has been faithfully restored.

Bike riders can be seen everywhere on the Iron Horse Trail.

ride takes you through mostly residential neighborhoods on a wide paved path. Only the busier streets you'll cross are listed here. Yield to traffic at intersections. While most motorists will yield the right-of-way, don't count on it.

Start riding at Walden Park, a small residential park north of downtown Walnut Creek. Contra Costa Canal/Walnut Creek Canal crosses here as well, making it an ideal location from which to start riding. The park has a children's playground, restrooms, and drinking fountains.

After crossing the Ygnacio Valley Road multi-use bridge you'll follow a canal through downtown Walnut Creek, right next to office buildings. Once past Newell Avenue the ride leaves office buildings, passes under Interstate 680, and then cuts through a broad open-space corridor in residential Alamo and Danville.

In downtown Danville you'll turn around at the Danville Railroad Museum, located at Railroad and Prospect avenues. The station was moved a short distance from Church Street and Railroad Avenue in the late 1990s. Completely restored in railroad yellow, it has been

MILEAGE LOG

0.0 Begin ride at Walden Park. Start mileage at crosswalk traffic light on Oak Road at Contra Costa Canal recreation path. Ride straight, going east, on the recreation path.

0.2 Right at stop sign onto Iron Horse Trail. 0.5 Walden Road stop sign. 1.1 Walnut Creek Elementary School on left.

1.2 Take recreation bridge over Ygnacio Valley Road. 1.8 Cross Mt. Diablo Boulevard.

2.3 Right on Newell Avenue, then immediate left onto path next to Main Street. Either use the left turn lane on Newell or cross Newell and stop at Main Street, riding south.

3.2 Keep right on path under Interstate 680. 3.32 Cross Danville Boulevard at traffic light.

3.34 Right against traffic on path.

3.36 Left to resume Iron Horse trail. 4.3 Drinking fountain. 5.0 Cross Ramona Way. Use caution here: Blind approach. 5.7 Cross Stone Valley Road.

8.4 Turn around at Danville Railroad Museum, the intersection of Railroad Avenue and Prospect Avenue. 11.1 Cross Stone Valley Road. 12.1 Cross Livorna Road. 12.5 Drinking fountain.

13.4 Right on Danville Boulevard.

13.5 Left at light to resume Iron Horse Trail. Keep left to ride under Interstate 680.

13.6 Left, continuing on trail next to Main Street.

14.6 Right on Newell to cross street, then continue north at crosswalk back onto Iron Horse Trail. 15.0 Cross Mt. Diablo Boulevard. 15.4 Civic Park on left. 15.5 Cross over Ygnacio Valley Road on recreation bridge.

16.7 Left on Contra Costa Canal Trail.

16.9 End ride at Walden Park.

45

transformed into a museum with old photos and paraphernalia from the railroad's early days in the late 1890s. A farmers' market takes place in a parking lot next to the museum on select weekends. California Pedaler bike shop is a block away on Church Street.

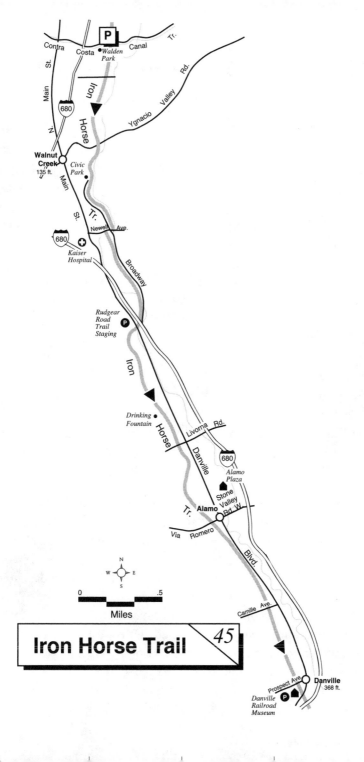

45

Iron Horse Trail 45

Lafayette-Moraga Regional Trail

DISTANCE >>> 14 miles

TERRAIN >>> Mostly flat

TRAFFIC >>> Light to moderate car traffic; bicyclists, hikers, in-line skaters

HOW TO GET THERE >>> If not by BART, take Interstate 580 to Highway 24 east, exiting in Orinda at the Moraga Way exit. Take BART back to Orinda.

THE BAY AREA RAPID TRANSIT system (BART) opens new dimensions in bike riding. It offers a fun, easy way to transport bikes without driving. Here's just one example: Take BART to the town of Orinda and loop back to the Lafayette BART station. The 14-mile ride follows Lafayette-Moraga Regional Trail, the former right-of-way of the Sacramento Northern Railroad. The paved path winds through a valley and a secluded canyon as it follows Las Trampas Creek. Bikes are permitted on BART all day on weekends and holidays, but check on restrictions during weekday peak commute hours.

Leave the Orinda BART station by the Moraga Way ramp and ride to Moraga, merging with traffic on Moraga Way under the Highway 24 overpass. The two-lane road has a broad shoulder all the way to the trail. There's a gradual 2.2-mile climb, followed by a descent to the town of Moraga.

At the traffic light, turn left onto Moraga Road. In less than half a mile there's another traffic light at St. Mary's Road, where you'll turn right and enter Moraga Commons Park to pick up the Lafayette-Moraga Trail. The park has a playground, restrooms, and drinking fountains.

Cross a wooden bridge and stay on the path for the next 5.8 miles. The trail originates about a mile to the south of the park.

The East Bay Regional Park Trail opened in 1976, after an interesting history. Mule trains once hauled redwood from Oakland to Sacramento; the route then became a right-of-way for the Sacramento Northern Railway. Sacramento Northern carried freight and passengers between San Francisco and Sacramento on electric trains from 1913 until 1941.

MILEAGE LOG

0.0 Start ride at the Orinda BART station, and take Moraga Way to the town of Moraga.

4.7 Left on Moraga Road at traffic light.

5.1 Right at traffic light at St. Mary's Road; immediately enter Moraga Commons Park and pick up the Lafayette-Moraga Trail. 9.9 Drinking fountain.

11.0 Left on Olympic Boulevard, exiting park. Immediately turn left onto Pleasant Hill Road at stop sign.

11.9 Left on Mt. Diablo Boulevard at traffic light.

13.6 Right on Happy Valley Road at traffic light (or right on Oak Hill Road at traffic light, then left on Deer Hill Road).

13.9 Right on Deer Hill Road to BART station. End ride.

46

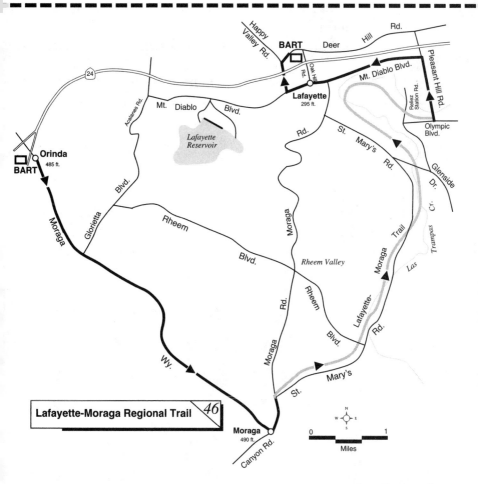

Lafayette-Moraga Regional Trail 46

The trail crosses driveways and some roads, where there are stop signs. Use caution crossing busy St. Mary's Road. The trail ends at a parking lot across from Reliez Station Road. On the far side of the parking lot, turn left on Olympic Boulevard and left again, riding north on Pleasant Hill Road.

Turn left on Mt. Diablo Boulevard and ride through downtown Lafayette. Turn right on Oak Hill Road at the traffic light, or right at Happy Valley Road, to reach BART.

Rails-to-Trails Conservancy, a national nonprofit organization based in Washington D.C., assists communities and organizations dedicated to preserving railroad right-of-ways for recreational use. More than 1,109 trails have been built on abandoned railroad corridors nationwide, totaling 11,311 miles.

The largest rail-to-trail project in the Bay Area is the San Ramon Valley Iron Horse Trail. Southern Pacific owned the rail line from the time it was established in the 1890s until it was abandoned in 1977. The trail has been added to this edition of *Bay Area Bike Rides;* see page 184.

46

San Mateo and Foster City Paths

47

DISTANCE >>> 14 miles

TERRAIN >>> Flat

TRAFFIC >>> Bicyclists, hikers, in-line skaters

HOW TO GET THERE >>> From Highway 101 north, take the Poplar Avenue exit. Turn right and go 2 blocks, turning right again on Humboldt. Go about a quarter-mile and turn right on Peninsula. Drive over the freeway and circle into the park. From Highway 101 south, take the Dore Avenue exit. Turn left onto North Bayshore Boulevard and go about half a mile before turning right again. It's about two-tenths of a mile to the park entrance kiosk. Entrance fee is $4. It's another half-mile to the end of the road, where there's ample parking in the Eucalyptus Group Picnic area behind the museum and next to Coyote Point Yacht Harbor.

ABOUT THE ONLY HILLS YOU'LL FIND in Foster City are freeway and waterway overpasses. Fortunately, developers of the city on the bay built miles of level, paved paths ideal for bicycling, if you're willing to put up with a little wind.

The recreation path linking San Mateo to Foster City gives a tantalizing preview of what the "Ring Around the Bay" will look like when it's finally completed. This path is part of the 250-mile bay trail plan developed by Senator Bill Lockyer in 1987. Although a completed trail is still years away, you can tour a 10-mile section named for Gerry Mon, a San Mateo engineer who was instrumental in having the trail built with federal and state transportation funds.

The ride starts in San Mateo at Coyote Point Park, identified by its rocky knoll and eucalyptus grove. This location has an interesting history as a recreation site. In 1922, Pacific City Amusement Park opened here to huge crowds. It was designed after New York's Coney Island; visitors rode a roller coaster, did the tango in a large dance hall, swam in the bay, sunbathed on a sandy beach, or dined in fine restaurants. Even with all these amenities, the multimillion-dollar project lasted only two years; once the initial excitement wore off, attendance dropped. A fire destroyed one-quarter of the grounds, and sewage in the bay closed the beach.

MILEAGE LOG

0.0 Start mileage at the beginning of the Gerry Mon Memorial Bike Path, dedicated by the city of San Mateo in 1987. A sign says SAN FRANCISCO BAY TRAIL. It's across the road from a one-ton boat anchor on display. **1.1** Cross San Mateo Creek. Watch for narrow barriers. **2.0** Cross the old East Third Avenue Bridge over Marina Lagoon. **3.9** Ride under Highway 92. The fishing pier parking lot is on the south side. Path continues south and west along Belmont Slough, then north along Marina Lagoon. **9.8** Ride under East Hillsdale Boulevard overpass and keep left.

10.8 Ride under Highway 92 overpass and then take first right on sidewalk into parking lot. Exit parking lot onto Fashion Island Boulevard on left. Take right turn from parking lot.

11.0 Left on Mariners Island Boulevard at traffic light.

12.0 Left on East Third Avenue at traffic light. Right onto recreation path, continuing north back to start.

14.2 End ride at Coyote Point Park.

Today's park has a clean, sandy beach, the bay water isn't so polluted, and you can still find a fancy restaurant (The Castaways) with a view of jets landing at San Francisco Airport. There's also an excellent nature museum, a golf course, and a marina.

The bike path starts from the marina on the bay and extends south to Foster City and Belmont Slough. You can ride at least 9 miles one way along the Bay, almost all the way around Foster City. A new East Avenue bridge over Marina Lagoon, finished in 1987, allowed the old bridge to be preserved for hikers and bicyclists.

Riding south (winds are usually northwesterly), you'll pass under the massive steel towers of San Mateo Bridge. The route offers sweeping views of the south bay and its salt ponds. The trail may be temporarily disrupted as improvements are made to Seal Point Shoreline Park.

Foster City was built around Brewer Island and 18 million cubic yards of landfill. Before the city was built, the island was part of a vast wetlands, which was gradually turned into salt ponds. The levees were

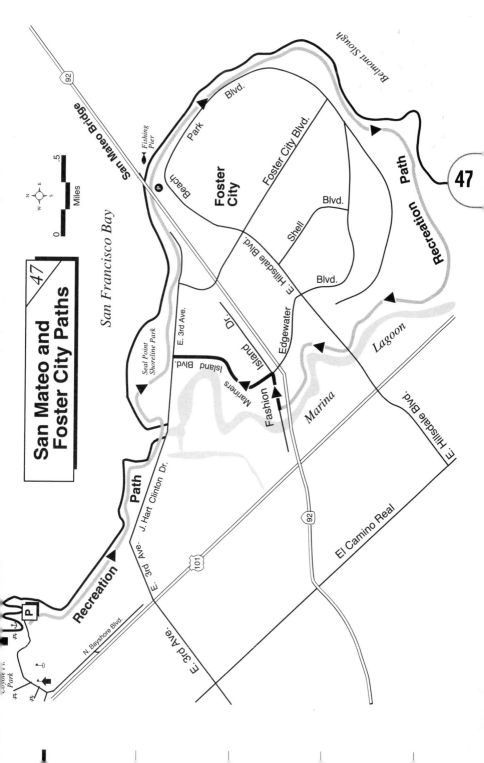

San Mateo and Foster City Paths

47

San Francisco Bay

San Mateo Bridge

Belmont Slough

Recreation Path

47

Foster City

Park Blvd.

Foster City Blvd.

Shell Blvd.

E. Hillsdale Blvd.

Blvd.

Beach

Fishing Pier

P

Edgewater

Lagoon

Marina

Seal Point Shoreline Park

E. 3rd Ave.

Island Dr.

Mariners Blvd.

Fashion Island Blvd.

Recreation Path

J. Hart Clinton Dr.

E. 3rd Ave.

N. Bayshore Blvd.

E. 3rd Ave.

101

92

92

El Camino Real

E. Hillsdale Blvd.

Coyote Pt. Park

P

N
W   E
S

0   .5

Miles

built to keep out the bay water, and without them Foster City would be a marsh.

This planned community was the dream of Texas oil man T. Jack Foster and Bay Area businessman Richard Grant. In 1959, they purchased the island from the Schilling and Leslie Salt companies. Construction began after a lengthy battle by environmentalists opposed to filling in the bay. A state bill was passed to create a municipal improvement district for governing the city. By 1964, some two hundred families lived in Foster City. Today, the city has twenty-eight thousand residents.

47

Sawyer Camp Trail

DISTANCE >>> 11 miles

TERRAIN >>> Flat

TRAFFIC >>> Bicyclists, hikers, in-line skaters

HOW TO GET THERE >>> From Interstate 280 north, exit at Hayne Road/Black Mountain Road west. Drive about a mile and a half south to the trailhead on Skyline Boulevard. Park along Skyline Boulevard. From the south, exit at Bunker Hill Drive and drive north about a mile and a half to the Crystal Springs Road trailhead.

48

SAWYER CAMP TRAIL IN SAN MATEO County isn't just popular, it's the Yellowstone Park of recreation paths. As many as 1,300 visitors flock to the narrow, paved path on a busy Sunday, more than 300,000 annually. The trail has another interesting distinction: It runs directly over the San Andreas Fault. Even without an earthquake, viewing pristine blue reservoirs along the trail can be a "moving" experience.

Start riding from the south entrance. The 8-foot-wide path follows the east shore of Crystal Springs Reservoir. There's usually a refreshing breeze and shade from oaks, buckeyes, and tan oak. Restrooms and a drinking fountain are located on the trail 3.4 miles from the south entrance, with picnic tables nearby. A short distance off the trail, don't miss seeing one of the oldest and largest bay laurel trees in the state. The Jepson laurel was named in honor of Willis Jepson, a California botanist.

North of the picnic grounds, the trail passes fern-covered slopes and a grove of bay trees giving welcome shade on hot summer days. Springs and a creek keep the area green year-round. You'll have a gradual climb to San Andreas Dam, followed by a steeper climb to the north entrance at Hillcrest Boulevard. Retrace the path or, if you're not bothered by cars, return on Skyline Boulevard as described in the Mileage Log.

Ride the trail midweek if you want to avoid the crowds, but early mornings on weekends aren't bad either. Obey the posted 10 mph speed limit, and always slow down for hikers. The San Francisco Water

MILEAGE LOG

0.0 Start mileage at the south access, at the Skyline Boulevard and Crystal Springs Road intersection. Parking is available on Crystal Springs Road. 3.4 Water, restrooms, picnic tables. Historic bay tree located 25 yards west of tables. 5.0 Top of San Andreas Dam. 5.9 North entrance to Sawyer Camp Trail at Hillcrest Boulevard. Return same way, or take frontage road back to Sawyer Camp Trail. Ride up the freeway ramp onto 280 heading south. (Yes, it's legal.) Stay on the walkway until ramp ends.

6.6 Take the Trousdale Drive exit. Immediately pick up the walkway.

6.7 Left on Trousdale Drive at stop sign.

6.8 Right on Skyline Boulevard at stop sign.

9.7 Right on Golf Course Road at stop sign, and ride under Interstate 280.

9.8 Left on Skyline Boulevard at stop sign.

11.1 Return to Sawyer Camp Trail. End ride.

Department closely monitors the water supply here; watershed land to the west of the reservoir is closed to the public.

Sawyer Camp Trail was a little-used dirt road until 1979, when the county paved it. The road's history goes back to the 1850s. Leander Sawyer kept an inn here to serve picnickers and raise prize circus horses. The valley road later became the main stagecoach route from Millbrae to Half Moon Bay.

The San Andreas Reservoir was built in 1869 to provide water for burgeoning San Francisco; in 1934, the Hetch Hetchy pipeline started bringing water from the Tuolumne River in the Sierra to San Andreas Lake and its neighboring dams to the south, Upper (1877) and Lower (1888) Crystal Springs reservoirs. All three dams withstood the 1906 earthquake.

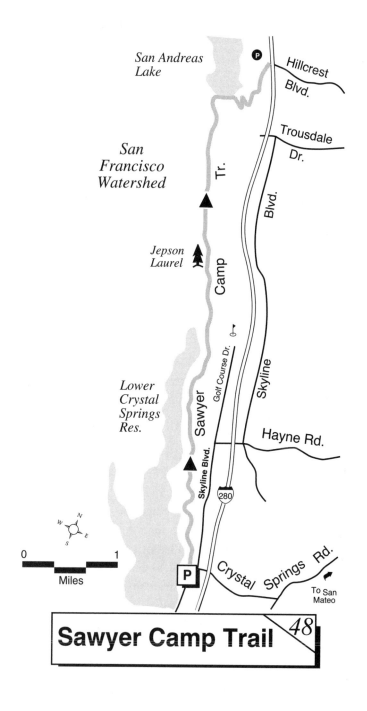

San Andreas
Lake

Hillcrest
Blvd.

Trousdale
Dr.

San
Francisco
Watershed

Tr.

Blvd.

Jepson
Laurel

Camp

Golf Course Dr.

Skyline

Lower
Crystal
Springs
Res.

Sawyer

Skyline Blvd.

Hayne Rd.

280

N
W   E
S

0   1

Miles

Crystal   Springs   Rd.

P

To San
Mateo

Sawyer Camp Trail *48*

Shoreline Park

49

- **DISTANCE** >>> 9 miles
- **TERRAIN** >>> Flat
- **TRAFFIC** >>> Bicyclists, pedestrians, in-line skaters
- **HOW TO GET THERE** >>> From Highway 101, take the Shoreline Boulevard exit north. Go straight for about 2 miles to the park entrance. Park at the entrance or at Shoreline Lake.

SHORELINE PARK, LIKE MANY PARKS bordering San Francisco Bay, occupies a former garbage dump. San Francisco buried its garbage here for more than thirteen years. The city of Mountain View used the $13 million in dumping fees to pay for the park. From the way it looks today, you'd never guess the park was once a dump. It's one of the premier parks on the bay for casual riding.

The city got more than just a beautiful park from the arrangement—it got methane, a byproduct of rotting garbage. The gas collection pays for park maintenance. The city capped the lengthy shoreline development project in 1986 by opening the Shoreline Amphitheatre, brainchild of the late Bill Graham. Top recording artists perform at this tent-shaped outdoor theater.

Most of the park offers a quiet, peaceful setting to be enjoyed while riding on recreation paths skirting the bay. This guide offers two routes. The longer ride takes you into the salt marshes on a dirt trail; the shorter ride follows Stevens Creek for a couple of miles.

In the center of the park there's a man-made lake with a boat launch, golf course, clubhouse, and the historic Rengstorff House. The Stevens Creek Trail ride starts at the boat launch. In the late fall, nearby salt ponds have some of the best duck watching anywhere in the Bay Area. Duck hunters still use duck blinds in the salt marsh. As the hunters shoot, bird watchers quietly stroll along on the levees. The park interior has ring-necked pheasant, but burrowing owls disappeared in the late 1980s.

The salt marsh ride starts from a parking lot inside the main entrance at the north end of Shoreline Boulevard and loops through

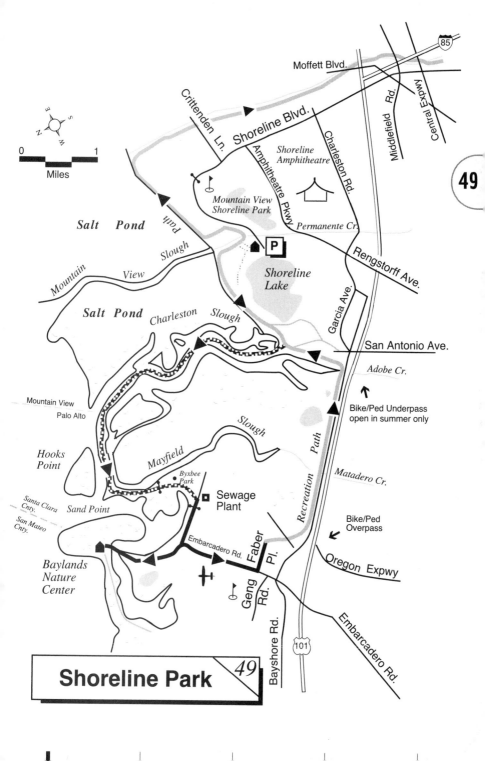

N
E · S · W

0   1
Miles

85

Moffett Blvd.

Crittenden Ln.

Shoreline Blvd.

Shoreline Amphitheatre

Amphitheatre Pkwy

Charleston Rd.

Middlefield Rd.

Central Expwy

49

Salt Pond

Slough
Path

Mountain View Shoreline Park

Permanente Cr.

Rengstorff Ave.

Mountain   View

P

Shoreline Lake

Garcia Ave.

Salt Pond

Charleston   Slough

San Antonio Ave.

Adobe Cr.

↑
Bike/Ped Underpass
open in summer only

Mountain View
Palo Alto

Slough

Recreation Path

Matadero Cr.

Hooks Point

Mayfield

Byxbee
Park

Sewage
Plant

Bike/Ped
Overpass
↙

Santa Clara
Cnty.

San Mateo
Cnty.

Sand Point

Embarcadero Rd.

Faber Pl.

Oregon   Expwy

Baylands Nature Center

Geng Rd.

Bayshore Rd.

101

Embarcadero Rd.

Shoreline Park   *49*

MILEAGE LOG
SALT MARSH RIDE

0.0 Start mileage at Shoreline Sailing Lake building, in front of the boat loading ramp. Ride north. Recreation path picks up after crosswalk. Take a right at the rock divider. After another 50 yards go left at the split in the recreation path, picking up Permanente Creek on your right.

0.7 Right at Y junction.

1.0 Right on dirt levee at pump house and portable restrooms. Marsh Loop Bay Trail heads into the salt marsh and returns to Palo Alto. 3.0 Cross spillway and then go left. 3.2 Walk bike through gate.

3.6 Right on Embarcadero Road at Palo Alto recycling center. Byxbee Park parking on left.

3.8 Keep straight at Embarcadero Road junction and stop sign. 4.3 Lucy Evans Baylands Nature Interpretive Center on left. Turn around and return by same road.

4.8 Right on Embarcadero Road at stop sign.

5.2 Left on Faber Place next to car dealership.

5.4 Right at end of Faber Place onto recreation path.

5.8 Left at frontage road, staying on recreation path.

7.3 Left on paved path immediately after crossing bridge over Adobe Creek.

7.7 Right at pump house on recreation path.

7.9 Left at Y intersection.

8.5 Right at junction. Left again at rock divider. End ride at boat house.

MILEAGE LOG
STEVENS CREEK RIDE

0.0 Start mileage in front of Rengstorff House sign at circular driveway. Left from parking lot onto paved road. Right again in 60 yards at crosswalk leading to recreation path. Keep straight and cross wooden bridge over Permanente Creek. 0.1 Keep left at next Y junction.

0.4 Left at unmarked T junction, continuing on recreation path.

1.4 Left at T junction. Go 50 yards and turn right at next T junction. 2.9 Ride under Highway 101.

3.3 Cross Moffett Boulevard at traffic light, continuing on recreation path. 3.6 Ride under Middlefield Avenue. 3.8 Keep straight at T junction, with bridge on left.

3.9 Left onto bridge over creek.

4.1 Right onto bridge over train tracks, Central Expressway and Evelyn Avenue.

4.3 Right back onto recreation trail.

4.4 Right onto bridge over creek, then immediate left, and keep left at next junction. Ride under overpass.

4.5 Trail ends at Landes Park. Turn around and go back the way you came.

Palo Alto baylands on salt pond levees. On the way to the levees you'll cross Permanente Creek on a wooden bridge. There's a pump house and a portable restroom where Marsh Loop Bay Trail, a dirt levee bordering Charleston Slough, begins. Turn right and ride north on the levee to Byxbee Park in Palo Alto. (Beware: the levee turns to a muddy quagmire in the rain or heavy winter fog.)

From the Byxbee Park entrance, turn right onto a paved road leading to a recycling center. Ride north to the Baylands Nature Center next to the airport. The center is built on concrete pilings over the salt marsh. Docents hold guided bike rides and walks, and give slide shows and movies about the bay.

49

Return to Embarcadero Road and turn right. Go 0.4 miles and turn left onto Faber Lane. Pick up the recreation path at the end of the street and head south. You'll cross Matadero Creek, Dry Creek, and then Adobe Creek before turning left and taking the path back to the pump station.

The Emily Renzil Wetlands on your left were reclaimed in 1993 by the city of Palo Alto. A path under Highway 101 next to Adobe Creek remains open during the dry season. Turn right at the pump house and retrace your route.

Coyote Creek Trail

DISTANCE >>> 30 miles round-trip

TERRAIN >>> Flat

TRAFFIC >>> Bicyclists, hikers, in-line skaters

HOW TO GET THERE >>> From Highway 101, take the Hellyer Road exit. Go west to the Hellyer Park entrance ($3 per car). Follow the signs to the Velodrome, on your right.

HERE'S A 30-MILE ROUND-TRIP ROUTE completely on recreation paths! It's the longest ride on a recreation path in the Bay Area, though soon to be surpassed by the Iron Horse Trail. You can start in south San Jose and ride to Morgan Hill, then retrace the route.

Begin riding from the Velodrome, Northern California's only bicycle racing track, located in Hellyer Park. The 336-meter concrete oval, built in 1962, is owned by Santa Clara County. The late Ed Steffani from Los Gatos designed and helped build the track. On Friday nights in the summer there's racing under the lights. But the crowds pale in comparison to San Jose track racing in the 1920s and 1930s, when race gambling was legal.

The path follows Coyote Creek under the shade of cottonwoods, sycamores, and oaks. San Jose retains a public right-of-way along most of the creek's 31 miles. Plans call for extending the trail the length of Coyote Creek from Anderson Reservoir to San Francisco Bay.

The path dips under the Hellyer Avenue bridge and then passes Cottonwood Lake on the left. The lake is stocked with trout

Coyote Creek County Park links San Jose with Morgan Hill.

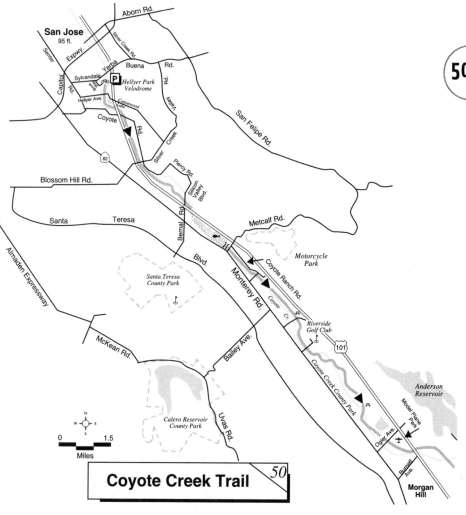

Coyote Creek Trail

50

MILEAGE LOG

0.0 Start mileage next to Hellyer Park Velodrome restrooms. Trail starts in about 50 yards, after crossing creek.

0.2 Keep straight at junction with bridge, crossing under Hellyer Avenue. Cottonwood Lake on left. 0.9 Ride under Highway 101. 2.4 Bridge on right.

3.0 Ride under new Silver Creek Valley Road bridge, then right onto old bridge crossing creek.

3.1 Left after crossing bridge to continue trail at gravel parking lot. Coyote Creek on left. 4.6 Cross under Silicon Valley Boulevard bridge. 5.5 Ride under Highway 101 (junction for Highway 85). 5.9 Left at junction with Metcalf Park at basketball court. Restrooms.

6.7 Left on recreation bridge. Right after crossing bridge. Parkway Lakes straight ahead. No state fishing license needed. Lake is stocked.

6.8 Cross Metcalf Road and pick up path.

7.7 Left onto Coyote Ranch Road.

7.8 Right at T junction. Gate.

7.9 Right back onto path next to dog training area. 8.6 Cross creek on trail at creek level. 9.6 Golf course.

10.6 Right, staying on path next to road; go 100 yards and turn left across road to continue on path. 11.4 Cross bridge over creek. 12.1 Eucalyptus rest area. 13.3 Model airplane club. 14.0 Ride under Highway 101.

14.9 Trail ends. Anderson Reservoir ranger station. Turn around and return same way.

29.8 End ride.

Bike racers speed around Hellyer Park's velodrome on Friday nights.

and bluegill, and there's a playground nearby for the kids. The 8-foot-wide trail follows Coyote Creek, normally placid, although it flooded in the early 1980s and wiped out a section of the trail. Industrial parks line the way everywhere along the trail, but Santa Clara Valley clings to a few parcels of its agricultural heritage nearby; orchards and vegetable fields mix with housing developments.

At 3.0 miles, ride under the new bridge and under Piercy Road Bridge. On the west side of the creek, the trail winds through orchards and past farmhouses.

50

The trail bisects land sandwiched between percolation ponds on the left and housing on the right. Next to Monterey Road (Highway 82), you'll take a recreation bridge and then cross Metcalf Road.

The newest stretch of 10-foot-wide path was finished in 1991 at a cost of $1 million and extends from a mile south of Metcalf Road to the Anderson Reservoir ranger station. The trail crosses a bridge and skirts the edge of a golf course. Picnic benches are conveniently located at several points along the path. Pass a gravel pit and then a model airplane park before riding under Highway 101.

Northwesterly winds can make the return trip a good deal more difficult.

Los Gatos Creek Trail

DISTANCE >>> Up to 16 miles

TERRAIN >>> Flat

TRAFFIC >>> Bicyclists, hikers, in-line skaters

HOW TO GET THERE >>> From Highway 17, take the Lark Avenue exit going north. After exiting, take a right at the traffic light onto Lark Avenue. In about a quarter-mile, turn left onto University Avenue. It's about a mile to reach Vasona Park. You can also take the Los Gatos–Saratoga exit going north and turn right on University Avenue.

SLOWLY BUT SURELY, LOCAL GOVERNments have combined resources to build a network of recreation paths along South Bay creeks. Los Gatos Creek Recreation Path has been lengthened in recent years to downtown Los Gatos. Someday it will join the Coyote Creek Recreation Path in San Jose. We can only dream about it right now, and must be content with an 8-mile path following Los Gatos Creek from Los Gatos to west San Jose.

Start the ride at Vasona County Park, just east of downtown Los Gatos, if you want to spend some time in a beautiful park afterwards. (You can also start at Williams School in San Jose, or at Campbell Park in Campbell.) The spacious Vasona County Park has a miniature steam train built in 1903, a historic carousel with lovingly restored antique horses, playgrounds, barbecue pits, food stands, and a lake with plenty of wildlife. Parking inside the park is scarce on busy weekends.

The path follows Los Gatos Creek, which flows year-round thanks to controlled releases at Lexington Reservoir. At the east end of Vasona Park, you'll ride around Vasona Lake dam, built in 1935 for flood control. Los Gatos Creek retains much of its natural beauty from downtown Los Gatos until joining the Guadalupe River in San Jose.

Continuing east, you'll pass Campbell Park on the left at the Campbell Avenue overpass. A Parcourse begins at the park and follows the Los Gatos Creek trail. There's a 1-mile stretch of paved path on the other side of the creek, next to a mobile home park. On weekends the trail attracts walkers, joggers, and in-line skaters.

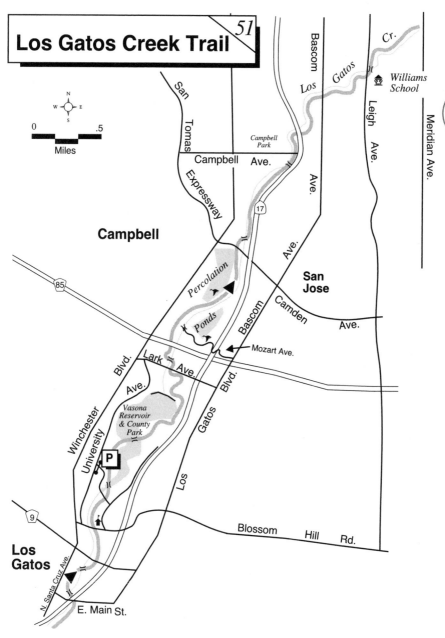

Los Gatos Creek Trail

51

51

N
W E
S

0 .5
Miles

Campbell

San Jose

Los Gatos

San Tomas Expressway

Bascom Ave.

Los Gatos Cr.

Williams School

Meridian Ave.

Leigh Ave.

Campbell Park

Campbell Ave.

17

85

Percolation Ponds

Camden Ave.

Bascom Ave.

Mozart Ave.

Lark Ave.

Winchester Blvd.

University Ave.

Vasona Reservoir & County Park

Los Gatos Blvd.

P

9

Blossom Hill Rd.

N. Santa Cruz Ave.

E. Main St.

MILEAGE LOG

0.0 Start mileage at the stop sign on the bike path at Meridian Avenue.

0.6 Right at bridge, then right again after crossing bridge. Williams School straight ahead. 0.7 Ride under Leigh Avenue. 1.3 Ride under Bascom Avenue. 1.5 Ride under bridge. 1.6 Ride under bridge. 1.9 Ride under Highway 17. 2.2 Ride under Campbell Avenue, followed by a bridge to Campbell Park on the right.

3.3 Right over bridge at waterfall. Left after bridge and chicane. 3.4 Ride under San Tomas Expressway. 3.7 Percolation ponds on right. 4.3 Bridge on left connects to bike path over Highway 17. 4.7 Ride under Highway 17.

5.2 Left over bridge and creek, then right after crossing creek. Ride under Lark Avenue. 5.6 Base of Vasona Reservoir, beginning short climb. 6.1 Keep right at junction. Restrooms on left.

6.3 Right over bridge, and left after crossing bridge.

6.5 Cross road and continue on trail. Sign says Meadowbrook Creekside Picnic Area.

6.8 Left at Wildcat Railroad crossing after crossing tracks. Right after crossing tracks. Right again in 25 yards, continuing along creek. 7.0 Ride under Blossom Hill Road. 7.1 Ride under Roberts Road. 7.6 Ride under Los Gatos–Saratoga Road. 7.9 Cross Miles Avenue. 8.0 Right over creek. 8.1 Left over creek and then right after crossing bridge. Trail turns to dirt at mill.

9.4 Steep hill. Left over Lexington Reservoir spillway.

9.6 Begin climb up Lexington Reservoir recreation path. 9.9 Top of dam. Return to start.

Farther along, you'll pass percolation ponds, a favorite gathering place for urban fishermen and hungry cormorants perched on phone wires. Everything from white-plumed egrets to coots and kingfishers feed at the ponds. At the west end of the percolation ponds, a path crosses the creek on the way to dirt trails and a bike/pedestrian bridge over Highway 17.

Going south, the path hugs the tree-lined Los Gatos Creek and then the Highway 17 sound wall before breaking into the open. Elevated wood-plank sections go right behind Old Town Mall. You'll cross the creek twice on multi-use bridges before reaching Forbes Mill. This impressive stone structure was built in 1854 by James Alexander

Forbes. The town that grew around the flour mill was first called Forbes Mill, then Forbestown, and finally Los Gatos.

From the mill, the dirt trail makes its way to Lexington Reservoir, following an abandoned railroad right-of-way. There's one short, steep hill on the way to the dam. A paved path cuts diagonally up the face of the dam.

The Mileage Log starts at the east end of the trail.

51

Bibliography

Anderson, Charles. *Mountain Bike Trails of the Bay Area*. Palo Alto, Calif.: Omega Printing, 1984.

Arrigoni, Patricia. *Making the Most of Marin: A California Guide*. Novato, Calif.: Presidio Press, 1981.

Beal, Richard A. *Highway 17*. Aptos, Calif.: The Pacific Group, 1991.

Butler, Phyllis Filiberti. *The Valley of Santa Clara, Historic Buildings, 1792–1920*. San Jose, Calif.: Junior League of San Jose, 1975.

Davis, Dorothy. *A Pictorial History of Pleasanton*. Pleasanton, Calif.: Pleasanton National Bicentennial Committee, 1976.

Emmanuels, George. *California's Contra Costa County, An Illustrated History*. Fresno, Calif.: Panorama West Books, 1986.

Futcher, Jane. *Marin, the Place, the People: Profile of a California County*. New York: Holt, Reinhart, Winston, 1981.

Graves, Al and Ted Wurm. *The Crookedest Railroad in the World*. Glendale, Calif.: Trans-Anglo Books, 1983.

Halley, William. *The Centennial Year Book of Alameda County*. Oakland, Calif.: 1876.

Hynding, Alan. *From Frontier to Suburb: The Story of San Mateo Peninsula*. Belmont, Calif.: Star Publishing Co., 1982.

Kneiss, Gilbert H. *Redwood Railways*. San Diego: Howell-North Press, 1956.

Koch, Margaret. *Santa Cruz County: Parade of the Past.* Fresno, Calif.: Valley Publishers, 1973.

Lewis, Oscar. *San Francisco: Mission to Metropolis.* San Diego: Howell-North Books, 1966.

MacGregor, Bruce and Richard Truesdale. *A Centennial: South Pacific Coast.* Boulder, Colo.: Pruett Publishing Co., 1982.

McCarthy, Frances Florence. *The History of Mission San Jose California 1779–1835.* Fresno, Calif: Academy Library Guild, 1958.

Neumann, Phyllis. *Sonoma County Bike Trails.* Penngrove, Calif.: 1978.

O'Hare, Carol. *A Bicyclist's Guide to Bay Area History.* Sunnyvale, Calif.: Fair Oaks Publishing, 1989.

Payne, Stephen M. *Santa Clara County, Harvest of Change.* Northridge, Calif: Windsor Publications, 1987.

Richards, Gilbert. *Crossroads, People and Events of the Redwoods.* Woodside, Calif.: Gilbert Richards Publications, 1973.

Sandoval, John. *The History of Washington Township.* Castro Valley, Calif.: 1985.

Stanger, Frank M. *Sawmills in the Redwoods*, San Mateo, Calif.: San Mateo County Historical Association, 1967.

Stanger, Frank M. *South from San Francisco*, San Mateo, Calif.: San Mateo County Historical Association, 1963.

State of California. *Geologic Guidebook of the San Francisco Bay Counties.* San Francisco: Division of Mines, 1951.

Tays, George, ed. *Historical Landmarks & Sites of Alameda County, California.* Oakland: Alameda County Library, 1938.

Town of Danville. *Danville, Portrait of 125 Years.* Alamo, Calif.: Robert Pease & Co., 1984.

Verardo, Denzil and Jennie Dennis. *Napa Valley, From Golden Fields to Purple Harvest.* Northridge, Calif.: Windsor Publications, 1986.

Whitnam, Dorothy L. *An Outdoor Guide to the San Francisco Bay Area.* Berkeley, Calif.: Wilderness Press, 1976.

Young, John V. *Ghost Towns of the Santa Cruz Mountains.* Santa Cruz, Calif.: Western Tanager Press, 1984.

Recommended Web Sites

Links are maintained on my Web site: www.geocities.com/rayhosler

MOUNTAIN BIKE

ALMADEN QUICKSILVER COUNTY PARK
www.parkhere.org/prkpages/aq.htm

ALPINE ROAD
Midpeninsula Regional Open Space District trail conditions: www.openspace.org/trails1.html
Windy Hill: www.openspace.org/windyh.pdf
Russian Ridge and Coal Creek Preserves: www.openspace.org/rridge.html

BOLINAS RIDGE
Bicycle Trails Council of Marin: www.btcmarin.org/old_site/home.html

BRIONES PARK
www.ebparks.org/parks/briones.htm#map

GAZOS CREEK ROAD
Big Basin Redwoods State Park: www.parks.ca.gov/central/santacruz/bbrsp406.htm
Sempervirens Fund: www.sempervirens.org

OLD HAUL ROAD
San Mateo County Parks: www.eparks.net/parks/Pescadero%20Creek/index.htm/

HENRY W. COE PARK
www.coepark.parks.ca.gov

JOSEPH D. GRANT COUNTY PARK
Santa Clara County Parks: www.parkhere.org/prkpages/grant.htm

LONG RIDGE
Midpeninsula Regional Open Space District: www.openspace.org/map3.
html

ROMP: www.romp.org

MIWOK TRAIL
Golden Gate National Recreation Area: www.nps.gov/goga

Bikeparts.com: www.bikeparts.com/trails/marin.html

MT. TAMALPAIS
History of the railroad: http://hunza1.tripod.com/tamalpais

State Park: www.cal-parks.ca.gov/north/marin/mtsp239.htm

PURISIMA CREEK ROAD
Midpeninsula Regional Open Space District map: www.openspace.org/
purisima.html

REDWOOD PARK
www.ebparks.org/parks/redwood.htm

Bicycle Trails Council of the East Bay: www.btceastbay.org

REPACK ROAD
Repack History by Joe Breeze: www.mtnbikehalloffame.com/history.
cfm?page=3

Point Reyes National Seashore: Marin Water District: www.marinwater.
org

SHELL RIDGE
Save Mount Diablo: www.savemountdiablo.org/historylink.htm

East Bay Regional Parks: www.ebparks.org/parks/brdiotr.htm

SOQUEL DEMONSTRATION FOREST
Ride reviews: www.mtbr.com/trails/california-bayarea/soqueldemon
strationforest.html

Trail workers: www.trailworkers.com/soquel_forest_.cfm

STEVENS CANYON
Stevens Creek County Park: www.parkhere.org/prkpages/stcrk.htm

ROAD

APTOS
History: www.aptoschamber.com/tourism/history.html

ATHERTON
History: www.ci.atherton.ca.us/history.html

BIG BASIN REDWOODS PARK
Big Basin Redwoods State Park: www.parks.ca.gov/central/santacruz/
    bbrsp406.htm
Boulder Creek Chamber of Commerce: www.boulder-creek.com/bc_
    locate.htm

CHILENO VALLEY
Petaluma Chamber of Commerce: www.petaluma.org/visitor

CLAYTON
Blackhawk Museum: www.blackhawkauto.org

GOLDEN GATE PARK
Travel guide: www.sfgate.com/traveler/guide/sf/neighborhoods/ggpark.
    shtml

HILLSBOROUGH
History: www.hillsborough.net/site/fhistory.html

MARIN HEADLANDS
U.S. Govt. site: www.nps.gov/goga/mahe/

MARTINEZ
New bridge: www.dot.ca.gov/dist4/route80r.htm
John Muir House: www.nps.gov/jomu
Carquinez Strait Scenic Drive: www.abag.ca.gov/bayarea/baytrail/
    vtour/map6/access/carquinz.htm

MORGAN HILL

Chesbro Reservoir: www.parkhere.org/prkpages/chesbro.htm

Uvas Reservoir: www.parkhere.org/prkpages/uvasres.htm

Chamber of Commerce: www.morganhill.org/mhcc/points.htm

MT. DIABLO

Mt. Diablo State Park: www.parks.ca.gov/central/bayarea/mdsp203.htm

MT. HAMILTON

Lick Observatory: www.ucolick.org/lickobs/index.html

Mt. Hamilton Challenge: www.hillsidegraphics.com/hamilton-challenge/
info.html

MUIR WOODS

Muir Woods National Monument: www.nps.gov/muwo

NAPA VALLEY

Bale Grist Mill: www.parks.ca.gov/north/silverado/bgm251.htm

Robert Louis Stevenson Park: www.parks.ca.gov/north/silverado/
rlssp215.htm

Hubcap Ranch: www.sonic.net/~laird/landmarks/counties/900-999/939_
napa.html

OLD LA HONDA ROAD

Palo Alto Bicycles: www.paloaltobicycles.com/ride6.html

Road gradient: www.graphics.stanford.edu/~lucasp/grade/oldlahonda.
html

POINT REYES

Point Reyes Seashore National Park: www.nps.gov/pore

Samuel P. Taylor State Park: www.parks.ca.gov/north/marin/sptsp233.
htm

PORTOLA VALLEY

Palo Alto Bicycles ride: www.paloaltobicycles.com/loopmap/loop.html

Stanford University map: www.stanford.edu/home/visitors/campus-map.html

SAN BRUNO MOUNTAIN

Save San Bruno Mountain: www.geocities.com/rainforest/canopy/4417

San Bruno Mountain Park: www.eparks.net/parks/sbmthome.htm

SAN FRANCISCO

San Francisco bike shops: www.rides.org/lv2options/lv4options/lv4brkes/san_francisco.html

Golden Gate Park: www.sfgate.com/traveler/guide/sf/neighborhoods/ggpark.shtml

SANTA CRUZ

Chamber of Commerce: www.santacruzca.org

Roaring Camp Railroad: www.roaringcamprr.com

SKYLINE BOULEVARD

East Bay Regional Parks: www.ebparks.org/parks.htm

Steam Train: http://hometown.aol.com/rvrytrain/index.html

Tilden Park: www.ebparks.org/parks/tilden.htm

SUNOL

Pacific Locomotive Association: www.ncry.org

TUNITAS CREEK ROAD

Woodside Store Museum: www.eparks.net/parks/woodhome.htm

CASUAL

COYOTE CREEK TRAIL
Hellyer Park Velodrome: www.usvh.com/NCVA
Coyote Creek Park: www.parkhere.org/prkpages/hellyer.htm

COYOTE HILLS REGIONAL PARK
Coyote Hills Regional Park: www.ebparks.org/parks/coyote.htm

IRON HORSE TRAIL
www.ebparks.org/parks/irontr.htm

LAFAYETTE-MORAGA REGIONAL TRAIL
Rails to Trails Conservancy: www.railtrails.org
Lafayette-Moraga Regional Trail: www.ebparks.org/parks/lafmotr.htm

LOS GATOS CREEK TRAIL
Los Gatos Creek Trail: www.parkhere.org/prkpages/lgcreek.htm
Vasona Park: www.parkhere.org/prkpages/vasona.htm
Billy Jones Wildcat Railroad: www.los-gatos.ca.us/los_gatos/parks_
    and_rec/billy_jones_rr/bjwrr.html

SAN MATEO AND FOSTER CITY PATHS
Bay Trail: www.abag.ca.gov/bayarea/baytrail/history.html
Coyote Point Museum: www.coyoteptmuseum.org

SHORELINE PARK
Shoreline Park: www.ci.mtnview.ca.us./shoreline/shoreline.html
Baylands Nature Center: www.city.palo-alto.ca.us/ross/baylands.html

Index